21 世纪高职高专规划教材·旅游与酒店管理系列

旅游英语

主　编　郭晓斌　尚季玲

副主编　刘冬阳　汤晓凤

参编者　蔡　琳　黄　玮　朱秀杰

中国人民大学出版社

·北京·

图书在版编目（CIP）数据

旅游英语/郭晓斌，尚季玲主编 . —北京：中国人民大学出版社，2012.12
21 世纪高职高专规划教材 . 旅游与酒店管理系列
ISBN 978-7-300-15946-1

Ⅰ.①旅… Ⅱ.①郭… ②尚… Ⅲ.①旅游—英语—高等职业教育—教材 Ⅳ.①H31

中国版本图书馆 CIP 数据核字（2012）第 261948 号

21 世纪高职高专规划教材·旅游与酒店管理系列
旅游英语
主　编　郭晓斌　尚季玲
副主编　刘冬阳　汤晓凤
参编者　蔡　琳　黄　玮　朱秀杰

出版发行	中国人民大学出版社		
社　　址	北京中关村大街 31 号	邮政编码	100080
电　　话	010 - 62511242（总编室）	010 - 62511398（质管部）	
	010 - 82501766（邮购部）	010 - 62514148（门市部）	
	010 - 62515195（发行公司）	010 - 62515275（盗版举报）	
网　　址	http://www.crup.com.cn		
	http://www.ttrnet.com（人大教研网）		
经　　销	新华书店		
印　　刷	山东高唐印刷有限责任公司		
规　　格	185 mm×260 mm　16 开本	版　次	2013 年 4 月第 1 版
印　　张	13.75	印　次	2013 年 4 月第 1 次印刷
字　　数	263 000	定　价	28.00 元

21世纪的今天，旅游业已经成为世界各国国民经济的重要组成部分，是世界上发展势头最强劲的产业之一，也是现代人日常生活的重要组成部分。就我国而言，公民的出境游和外国游客来华游的人数呈逐年上升的趋势。

在这种形势下，用英语向外国游客介绍我国悠久的历史文化和秀丽的山水，或在异国他乡与外国人进行交流沟通、深入了解异域文化，掌握旅游业的基本英语知识，显得十分必要。根据多年从事旅游工作和旅游教学的经验，我们精心编写了这本《旅游英语》教材，以期为较快提高旅游专业学生和旅游从业人员的英语水平提供一定的帮助。

本教材以旅游活动的整个过程为主线，选取了多个符合旅游活动流程的典型工作场景，密切贴合旅游业的核心工作轨迹，其所涉及的工作流程和服务理念特别适合旅游专业学生和旅游业从业人员的需求。本教材分为旅游业介绍、旅游服务和旅游文化三大部分，共十二章，内容涵盖旅游活动中的食、住、行、游、购、娱等各个方面。每一章包含引言、情景对话、专业词汇短语、阅读材料、技能练习和知识扩展等内容。

引言 包括本章简介、教学目标和背景知识，以帮助读者快速了解本章的主题和相关背景，以及本章要达到的知识和能力目标。

情景对话 选取了多个旅游活动场景，真实再现旅游服务过程，有利于读者快速熟悉旅游业工作流程和掌握旅游服务常用语。

专业词汇短语 大量补充和本章内容相关的词汇及常用表达方式，对读者扩充词汇量和提高口语表达能力有非常大的帮助。

阅读材料 与本章主题相关的文章，既可扩大词汇量和提升英语阅读能力，又可加深对国内外旅游业的历史和文化的了解。

技能练习 词汇、翻译练习部分可巩固本章所学知识，并提高读者对所学内容的应用能力；对话练习部分是对读者旅游英语口语能力的强化。

知识扩展 主要引入与本章相关案例研究、旅游业最新发展动态和发展思路、成功案例展示等，知识性和趣味性兼具，有利于增加读者的阅读兴趣。

本书由郭晓斌和尚季玲担任主编，刘冬阳和汤晓凤担任副主编，蔡琳、黄玮和朱秀杰参与编写。具体的编写分工为：郭晓斌（郑州铁路职业技术学院）编写第二章、第八章；尚季玲（郑州铁路职业技术学院）编写第三章、第五章；刘冬阳

（郑州牧业工程高等专科学校）编写第四章、第十二章；汤晓凤（河南省轻工业学校）编写第九章；蔡琳（郑州铁路职业技术学院）编写第六章；黄玮（北京商贸学校）编写第七章、第十章；朱秀杰（郑州铁路职业技术学院）编写第一章、第十一章。

由于编者水平有限，疏漏和不足之处在所难免，恳请读者不吝指正。

郭晓斌　尚季玲

目 录
Contents

Chapter 1

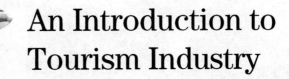

An Introduction to Tourism Industry

Part Ⅰ Lead-in

【本章简介】

本章主要对旅游产业进行总体概述。读者通过情景对话以及延伸阅读了解旅游产业的定义和构成、旅游产品的特点，最后通过练习进一步掌握与旅游产业有关的知识。

【教学目标】

1. 掌握与旅游产业相关的专业词汇及用语；
2. 熟悉旅游产业的构成要素；
3. 了解旅游产品的文化知识；
4. 能够简要阐述旅游产业的特点。

【背景知识】

作为服务行业，旅游业是由许多有形和无形的要素构成的。旅游业的有形要素包括交通和住宿等；旅游业的无形要素主要与旅游者的旅游动机、旅游目的以及旅游体验相关，比如通过旅游结识新朋友、体验新文化或者经历一次冒险等。旅游业在许多国家是一个动态且具有前瞻性的产业。

Part Ⅱ Situational Dialogues

 Dialogue One

The Tourism Industry

A：We all know that tourism is one of the world's fastest-growing industries as well as the major source of foreign exchange earning and employment in many coun-

tries. Now, I'd like you to think and define the tourism industry ... Yes, Mary?

B: In my opinion, tourism industry is a comprehensive international industry that aims to provide facilities and services for people traveling away from home, and it is at the same time, a type of foreign relations work.

A: OK. Yes, John? What's your understanding about tourism industry?

C: Well, there is some truth in what Mary just said. However, as far as I am concerned, tourism industry is the business of providing tours and services for travelers. It is closely relevant with businesses such as transportation, accommodation, food and beverage, tourist attractions, travel agencies and so on.

A: Very good. Both Mary and John have given the right answers. The tourism industry is a complex industry and therefore includes a number of different elements and organizations which work together.

Notes

1. comprehensive   *adj.* 综合的，复杂的
2. provide for   供养，提供
3. facility   *n.* 设备，工具
4. transportation   *n.* 交通
5. accommodation   *n.* 住宿
6. food and beverage   餐饮
7. tourist attractions   景点
8. travel agencies   旅行社
9. element   *n.* 要素，元素

 **Dialogue Two**

The Structure of the Tourism Industry

A: Could you tell us something about the structure of the tourism industry, sir?

B: Well, as we know, the tourism industry is a massive business chiefly made up of the three indispensable components: tourism resources, tourism facilities, and travel services.

A: Thank you, sir. But what do tourism resources, tourism facilities, and travel services refer to?

B: Tourism resources indicate tourist attractions. Tourism facilities refer to fixtures and devices for tourism industry. Travel services are services specially supplied for tourists.

A: Hmm, sir, do you mean that tourism industry cannot exist without the three elements?

B: Yes, absolutely. Tourist attractions are the basical things that make people become tourists, such as natural or historical scenery. When people travel, they need vehicles to transport them, hotels to accommodate them and restaurants to feed them. During traveling, people also require services offered by tour guides, hotels and restaurants.

A: Thank you, sir. Are the services supplied by the tour guides the most important part of travel services done by travel agencies?

B: Yes, very good. To be specific, travel agencies, accommodation operators and transport operators are the three key organizations that are likely to be involved in any traveling, which work together to form what is called as a distribution chain.

A: Thank you very much!

Notes

1. massive   *adj.* 厚重的，大块的，巨大的

2. indispensable components   不可或缺的成分

3. tourism resources   旅游资源

4. tourism facilities   旅游设施

5. travel services   旅游服务

6. accommodation operators   住宿运营商

7. transport operators   交通运营商

8. involve in   陷入，卷入；涉及

9. distribution chain   分销链

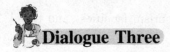 **Dialogue Three**

Tourism Industry Products

A：Accommodation is a key requirement for tourists, isn't it?

B：Sure. It plays an essential role in people's traveling.

A：Do you know what types of rooms are usually available in hotels?

B：Er, I think single rooms, twin rooms, double rooms are more popular among tourists. In addition, family rooms and suites are normally provided in hotels.

A：Are there other services supplied by hotels?

B：Good question. Laundry service, swimming pool, games rooms, meals and so on are also provided in larger hotels.

A：Is transport another key product of tourism industry?

B：Yes, you are right. Water transportation, air transportation and land transportation are the elements developed by transport operators.

A：Thank you.

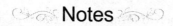 **Notes**

1. single rooms　单人房
2. twin rooms　双人房
3. double rooms　双人房
4. family rooms　家庭式旅馆
5. suite　*n.* 套房
6. laundry service　洗衣服务
7. water transportation　水运
8. air transportation　空运
9. land transportation　陆运

 **Dialogue Four**

Tourists of the Tourism Industry

A：Could you name the different types of tourists according to the services provided by the tourism industry?

B：I'm sorry.

A：Well，please have a try. Just think about the services provided by the tourism industry.

B：Er…I think there are domestic tourists，outbound tourists and incoming tourists，right?

A：Very good. Could you give us examples about each type of tourists?

B：OK. Imagine that a Chinese tourist who is traveling from China to America，he or she is an outbound tourist. If the Chinese tourist is traveling from his or her home to a destination elsewhere in China，he or she is a domestic tourist. While a tourist who is visiting China from America，he or she is a incoming tourist.

A：Absolutely right!

B：Thank you.

Notes

1. domestic tourist　国内游客
2. outbound tourist　出境游客
3. incoming tourist　入境游客

Part Ⅲ　Vocabulary & Useful Expressions

itinerary　*n.*　旅行计划

sightseeing　*n.*　游览

travel industry　旅游业

guide book　旅行指南

guide practice　导游实践

international tourism　国际旅游业

multilingual guide　会多种语言的导游

local guide　地陪

national guide　全陪

tour leader　领队

low season　淡季

season-low　淡季

slack season　淡季

off-peak season　淡季

off season　淡季

season-high　旺季

selling season　旺季

on season　旺季

peak season　旺季

receiving country　旅游接待国

tourist association　旅游协会

tourist authority/office　旅游局

tourist destination　旅游目的地

tourist organization　旅游组织

tourist spots　旅游点

World Tourism Day　世界旅游日

World Tourism Organization　世界旅游组织

Tourist Administration　旅游局

China's National Tourism Administration　中国国家旅游局

Provincial Tourism Administration　省旅游局

Municipal Tourism Administration　市旅游局

County Tourism Administration　县旅游局

Part Ⅳ　Reading Materials

Passage One

World Travel and Tourism Industry

Tourism was among one of the worst hit sectors during the global financial crisis.

As the world economy now heads toward recovery, the world tourism industry is also picking up with a faster-than-expected pace.

The tourism industry has long been regarded as a source for economic growth and employment. Incentives are high for many countries to ramp up their tourism industry as they try to get their economy back on track. It's hardly surprising that mega international events are being pursued globally, which is widely believed to catalyze the tourism industry. But despite its promising future, tourism remains vulnerable to factors like rising fuel prices, extreme weather and natural events and outbreak of epidemics as well. The Icelandic volcanic ash cloud which forced European aviation transport to a halt provides a reminder that people need to brace for similar incidents down the road.

Like the global economy, the emerging markets have again injected new impetus to the tourism industry. The World Tourism Organization estimates that China is expected to become the world's most popular tourism destination in 7 years. So what makes China get there in 7 years? How can we make progress in international cooperation and dodge the incidents that may partially strangle the tourism industry?

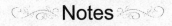

Notes

1. catalyze   *v.* 催化
2. epidemics   *n.* 泛滥，蔓延
3. tourism destination   旅游目的地

Passage Two

A Brief Introduction to China's Tourism Industry

Ever since the policy of opening and reform was adopted in 1978, the tourism industry in China, thanks to the great importance attached by the governments at various levels, has become a new but a most dynamic and most potentially strong sector in China's tertiary industry. In many parts of the country, tourism has been regarded as a pillar, superior or priority industry in promoting local economic development. The position of tourism in the national economy continues to be enhanced and upgraded.

In 2002, China ranked the fifth in the world in terms of both overnight tourist arrivals and tourism receipts in foreign exchange. In 2003, China continued to rank the fifth in the world in terms of overnight tourist arrivals, but due to the impact of SARS, China ranked the seventh in terms of tourism receipts in foreign exchange. China's domestic tourism was among the world's biggest, fastest-growing and most potentially strong markets; meanwhile, China's outbound tourism also saw steady development with each passing year. From 1996 to 2002, the total receipts of China's tourism has been growing by an annual average of 2-digit numbers for seven consecutive years, which is far above the average GDP growth rate of the same period, and has thus become a new growth point in the national economy of the country.

The tourism development of China has improved the investment environment, intensified the opening to the outside world, and helped the growth of related industries. It has played an active role in increasing internal demand and employment, in enhancing the structural readjustment and inter-regional economic link, and in assisting people in the poor areas to get rid of poverty and live a better life. Moreover, it has greatly promoted the economic prosperity and social development of China and the friendly exchanges between the Chinese people and the peoples of the world.

Notes

1. tertiary industry   第三产业
2. structural readjustment   结构调整

Part Ⅴ   Skill Training

Ⅰ. Matches.

a. slack season   1. 游览
b. selling season   2. 旅游目的地
c. travel services   3. 淡季
d. travel industry   4. 旅游点
e. multilingual guide   5. 第三产业

f. tour leader

g. sightseeing

h. tourist spots

i. tertiary industry

j. tourism destination

6. 旺季

7. 旅游服务

8. 旅游业

9. 会多种语言的导游

10. 领队

Ⅱ. Choices.

| attractions | service | domestic | tourism | dynamic | industry |
| destination | massive | accommodation | transport | | |

1. As a _____ industry, tourism has numerous tangible and intangible elements.

2. China's _____ tourism was among the world's biggest, fastest-growing and most potentially strong markets.

3. _____ was among one of the worst hit sectors during the global financial crisis.

4. The tourism _____ has long been regarded as a source for economic growth and employment.

5. The World Tourism Organization estimates that China is expected to become the world's most popular tourism _____ in 7 years.

6. The tourism industry is a _____ business chiefly made up of the three indispensable components.

7. To be specific, travel agencies, accommodation operators and _____ operators are the three key organizations that are likely to be involved in any traveling.

8. Tourist _____ are the basical things that make people become tourists, such as natural or historical scenery.

9. _____ is a key requirement for tourists, which plays an essential role in people's traveling.

10. Tourism is one of the most _____ and prosperous industries in many countries.

Ⅲ. Translate the following sentences into Chinese.

1. Tourism industry is a comprehensive international industry that aims to provide facilities and services for people traveling away from home.

2. Tourism resources indicate tourist attractions. Tourism facilities refer to fix-

tures and devices for tourism industry.

3. Tourist attractions are the basical things that make people become tourists, such as natural or historical scenery.

4. Water transportation, air transportation and land transportation are the elements developed by transport operators.

5. The tourism development of China has improved the investment environment, intensified the opening to the outside world, and helped the growth of related industries.

Ⅳ. **Translate the following expressions into English.**

1. The tourism industry is a massive business chiefly made up of the three indispensable components: _____, _____ and _____ (旅游资源、旅游设施和旅游服务).

2. 世界旅游组织

3. 会多种语言的导游

4. 旅游接待国

5. 中国国家旅游局

Ⅴ. **Oral practice.**

1. Please give a brief introduction about Chinese tourism industry.

2. In your opinion, which type of transport is most popular among tourists and why?

Part Ⅵ   Knowledge Expansion

旅游服务礼仪

世界旅游业的竞争焦点已从硬环境竞争转变到软环境竞争。旅游从业人员的职业道德、客我关系的处理、职业形象设计、行业礼貌语言等方面的礼仪修养是旅游的软环境，被认为是旅游业形象的灵魂。所以旅游服务礼仪在旅游业中占据了极为重要的地位。

旅游服务礼仪就是指旅游从业人员在旅游服务活动中向客人提供服务时所遵从的

对他人表示尊重与友好的行为规范和准则。旅游服务礼仪的内容主要是通过旅游从业人员良好的仪容、仪表、仪态，规范得体的礼貌服务用语及标准的服务操作程序，亲切的笑脸、耐心的态度、细致而周到的体贴与关怀来体现的。

旅游服务礼仪可分为三种形式：一是语言性礼仪，即各种旅游服务场合中的礼貌用语，如"您好"、"谢谢"、"再见"、"对不起"等，这些语言体现了对对方的尊敬、爱护和友好。二是行为体态性礼仪，即仪容、仪表、举止等，如鞠躬、敬礼、微笑、握手、拥抱、点头、敬酒等，这些行为体态体现了对对方的关怀和敬意。三是回避性礼仪，即在旅游服务接待过程中，谈话内容不要涉及疾病、死亡等不愉快的话题及女性的年龄、婚否等私事，别人反感的话避开不讲，别人反感的事避开不做，等等。为此，旅游从业人员必须了解各国的国情和民俗，了解旅游者的生活方式、饮食习惯以及爱好和忌讳。

旅游服务礼仪的准则是旅游从业人员在服务进程中处理与服务对象关系的出发点和行为规范。我们不仅需要学习和掌握礼仪的规则，而且需要懂得和遵循旅游服务礼仪的准则，从而提高服务质量。旅游服务礼仪的准则包括以下两个方面：

第一，尊重的准则。在旅游服务接待过程中必须尊重客人的人格尊严，尊重是礼仪的情感基础。无论客人的年龄大小、职务高低，都应一视同仁，不能看客施礼。旅游服务人员在工作中会接触到各种不同身份和地位的客人，要特别注意不能厚此薄彼。

第二，遵守的准则。礼仪是为了维护社会生活的稳定而形成和发展的，反映了全社会共同的利益和要求，社会上每一个成员都必须自觉遵守。旅游服务礼仪是旅游从业人员在旅游服务过程中所必须遵守的行为规范。旅游从业人员在为客人服务时必须自觉地遵守。如果违背了旅游服务礼仪规范，必然会影响旅游企业的形象，使旅游企业受到损失。所以旅游从业人员要不断提高职业道德、完善服务态度和提高服务质量。

Chapter 2

At the Travel Agency

At the Travel Agency

Part I   Lead-in

【本章简介】

　　旅行社在推动旅游消费、增加社会就业、促进人们交流等方面发挥着积极作用。具体来说，旅行社在满足人们旅游消费需要、实现旅游生产和旅游消费目的方面承担着非常重要的参谋作用，作为纽带和桥梁对旅游消费和生产起到积极的推动作用。读者通过对本章的学习，了解旅行社对于旅游产业的重要作用，并掌握相关的基础知识。

【教学目标】

1. 掌握旅游景点等特定名称的英语表达方式；
2. 学会在旅行社询问和介绍旅游信息，提高英语交际能力；
3. 了解有关北京和上海的新信息、新发展；
4. 学会如何查找、处理和利用与某一主题相关的信息，培养信息能力；
5. 初步学会设计旅游计划，提高与人合作的能力。

【背景知识】

　　旅行社组合生产的旅游产品和组织的团体旅游活动，往往是一个国家、一个地区旅游消费的先导，发挥着重要的引导、示范作用，很多新的旅游项目就是通过旅行社的宣传、推介、销售而进入人们的旅游消费中的。旅行社以其专业、便捷、高效的旅游产品、信息和组织接待服务，让绝大部分没有旅游经历和经验的人进入旅游消费过程。

　　就我国来说，旅游进入大众消费是改革开放之后的事，在这个快速兴起和大规模发展的阶段，旅行社组织的团队旅游一直是居民消遣性旅游的主要方式，至今在我国居民出境旅游中也仍然是主要方式。

　　正是在沟通旅游生产供给与消费需求的过程中，旅行社了解、掌握了旅游生产供给和消费需求的信息，成为最及时、最全面的旅游生产供给和消费需求信息的占有者和提供者。通过对这些信息资源的分析，旅行社就理所当然地成为旅游资源开发、宣传营销和居民出游计划、线路、目的地选择等旅游消费的参谋与得力助手。

Part II Situational Dialogues

Dialogue One

（At the Information Desk of a travel agency. ）

（A＝agent   W＝Mr. Wu）

A：Good morning，sir. Can I help you?

W：I'd like to spend my holidays abroad.

A：Yes，sir. What place would you like to see?

W：I have no idea. I'm just bored with my hard work and want to relax.

A：Maybe you can take your vacation in Switzerland. You may enjoy skiing.

W：But it's too cold，I prefer warm places.

A：Then what about Australia?

W：What is it like?

A：Lovely. There is a lot of sunshine there all year round.

W：Could you give me some other suggestions on what places to see?

A：Maybe you'll like the West Coast，L. A. ，and San Francisco.

W：What's there to see?

A：Hollywood，Universal Studios and Disneyland in L. A.

W：How is San Francisco?

A：It's probably the most beautiful town in the U. S. —all those hills, the bay, attractive old Victorian houses，and cable cars.

W：Thank you for your advice.

∽ Notes ∽

1. agency   *n.* 代理处

2. abroad   *adv.* 在国外，到国外

3. agent   *n.* 代理人，代理商

4. bored   *adj.* 厌烦的，厌倦的

5. relax   *v.* （指人）放松，轻松

6. vacation *n.* 假期

7. ski *v.* 滑雪

8. sunshine *n.* 阳光

9. suggestion *n.* 建议

10. bay *n.* 海湾

11. cable car 缆车

12. advice *n.* 劝告，忠告

 **Dialogue Two**

（L＝Li Ming　J＝Steve Johnson）

L：Good morning. This is China International Travel Service. What can I do for you?

J：Good morning. Can I speak to Mr. Li Ming?

L：This is Li Ming speaking.

J：Well，hello，Mr. Li. This is Steve Johnson. I have some friends who will come to China next Monday from Ann Arbor，Michigan to attend a package tour organized by your agency.

L：Yes，that's right. I am responsible for the organization of their trip in China.

J：Right. They want me to discuss some details with you.

L：Fine.

J：I'd like to go over with you the arrangement of the trip.

L：OK. After they have arrived on the morning of the August 16th，we will go directly to the hotel，check in and have lunch there. In the afternoon，we shall go to the Beijing Zoological Park and see the giant pandas there.

J：Wonderful. I believe the group members will love that.

L：We will leave pretty early on the 17th for the Great Wall at Badaling. It will be a two-hour bus trip. We will climb the Great Wall and have lunch there.

J：That should be interesting.

L：I believe so. In the evening，they will see a performance of Beijing Opera.

J：What about the 18th?

L：We shall visit the renowned Palace Museum with its different halls，its clock and watch exhibition，and the treasure halls. As it is the largest building complex in the

旅游英语

world，we will spend the whole morning there.

J：Excellent. I will telephone my friends and tell them the details. I am sure they will be very pleased. Bye.

L：Bye-bye.

❦ Notes ❦

1. package tour　包办旅行，包价旅游，跟团旅游

2. arrangement　*n.* 安排

3. zoological　*adj.* 动物的，动物学的

4. performance　*n.* 表演，演出

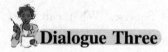Dialogue Three

Booking an Air Ticket

(C＝clerk　J＝Emily Johnson)

C：China Travel Service. Can I help you?

J：Yes，this is Mrs. Emily Johnson. I am calling to inquire what flights there are between Beijing and Hong Kong on August 1st.

C：Hold on，please. I will have a look. We have three flights between Beijing and Hong Kong on August 1st，one in the morning，one in the afternoon and one in the evening.

J：Good. Are there any seats left for the afternoon flight? My friend will arrive in Beijing on the morning of August 1st.

C：I am sorry，Mrs. Johnson. All seats are booked for the afternoon flight. How about the evening flight?

J：What time does it depart?

C：It departs at 19：45.

J：OK. That's fine. By the way，how much is the ticket?

C：A one-way ticket to Hong Kong from Beijing is 1,800 RMB yuan.

J：Can I make a reservation of one ticket of that flight?

C：Yes. May I have your friend's name?

20

J : Yes. Her name is Lisa McCarthy. When can you get the ticket ready?

C: Tomorrow morning.

J : Can you deliver it to my hotel?

C: Sure. Please tell me the specific address.

J : Room 545, Minzu Hotel.

C: OK. I have taken it down. See you tomorrow.

J : See you then and thank you very much.

Notes

1. inquire   *v.* 询问
2. flight   *n.* 航班
3. depart   *v.* 出发
4. reservation   *n.* 保留，预约，预订
5. deliver   *v.* 递送
6. specific   *adj.* 具体的，确切的，明确的

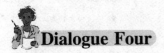 **Dialogue Four**

Booking a Passage

Clerk: Good morning, sir and madam. Can I help you?

Mr. Smith: Good morning. Will there be any ship sailing for Yantai next week?

Clerk: Yes, there's one next Monday.

Mr. Smith: Good. Can we book a cabin for two?

Clerk: Let me see. Ah, yes, how about this cabin? (Pointing to the plan.)

Mrs. Smith: That's OK.

Clerk: Please fill out this card.

Mr. Smith: (After filling it out.) Here you are.

Clerk: Please sit here for a moment. I will make out the tickets.

Mr. Smith: Thank you.

Clerk: Here are your tickets and that'll be 1,000 yuan. If there should be any last-minute change in the sailing time, we'll contact you by calling you at the telephone

number you have left us.

Mrs. Smith：Thanks.

Clerk：You are welcome. Have a good day.

Mr. and Mrs. Smith：You too.

Notes

1. book a passage　预订乘船旅行，订购船票
2. cabin　*n.* 船舱，客舱
3. plan　*n.* 平面图，设计图
4. last-minute change　临时变化

Part Ⅲ　Vocabulary & Useful Expressions

Ⅰ. Useful Words

excursion　*n.* 游览，短途旅行

manuscript　*n.* 手稿

sightseeing　*n.* 观光

castle　*n.* 城堡

church　*n.* 教堂

landscape　*n.* 风景

monument　*n.* 纪念碑

pagoda　*n.* 古塔

scenery　*n.* 风景

statue　*n.* 雕像

view　*n.* 景色

waterfall　*n.* 瀑布

a long journey　长途旅行

air travel　航空旅游

conducted/guided tour　有导游的旅游

group inclusive tour　包价旅游

independent/do-it-yourself travel　自助游

international tourism　国际旅游业

normal/luxury tour（travel）　标准/豪华游

outbound/inbound tourism　出境游/国内游

travel abroad　出国旅游

honeymoon trip　蜜月旅行

wedding classic travel vacation　婚假

wedding travel　旅行结婚

hot travel route/spot　黄金线路/景点

domestic tourism　国内旅游业

golden week for tourism　旅游黄金周

guide book　旅行指南

on business　因公

star grade hotel　星级宾馆

standard room　标准间

tourist guide　导游

business center　商业中心

cultural heritage　文化遗产

hot spring　温泉

natural scenery　自然风光

place of interest　名胜

places of historical interest　古迹

summer resort　避暑胜地

tourist attraction　景点

Ⅱ. Useful Expressions

1. Good morning. Can I help you?
   早上好。需要什么帮助吗?

2. I'd like to create a travel itinerary.
   我想做个旅行计划。

3. Where do you want to go?
   请问您想去哪儿?

4. I have no idea.
   没想好。

5. I hope to visit the seaside.
   我希望游览海滨城市。

6. Sure, how about Qingdao?

好的，青岛怎么样？

7. Right now is the best time of the year to visit Dalian.

现在是去大连的最好季节。

8. I've been there before.

我以前去过那里。

9. I think a southern city is better.

我想最好是去个南方城市。

10. How about Sanya?

三亚呢？

11. Blue sea, soft sand and gentle breezes.

蓝色的大海，软软的沙滩，柔和的微风。

12. Sounds really relaxing/great.

听起来不错。

13. Do you have any brochures?

有介绍资料吗？

Part Ⅳ   Reading Materials

 **Passage One**

Book a Passage

Traveling by sea is a very convenient and economical way of traveling. It is more relaxing, comfortable and cheaper than traveling by airplane or by train.

On some luxurious ships, there are various living and entertaining facilities, like restaurants, bars, theaters and even swimming pools, etc. The disadvantage of traveling by sea is that the speed is comparatively slow and some passengers are likely to be seasick with high wind.

Booking a passage is just like booking an airplane ticket. The travelers can go to the agencies or just telephone them to book a passage. As traveling by sea is greatly influenced by the weather situations, there may be some changes of the sailing time. The agency clerks are responsible for informing the passengers of such changes. For the convenient contact with passengers, the clerks will ask passengers to write down the detailed personal information like name, address and telephone number, etc. Also, they will show the passengers a printed plan of all the cabins with different classes, direction, etc., so that passengers can choose the cabins they like. The boat-trains can take the passengers to the port in time. Passengers only need to go to the appointed station on time and get on the train with the ship tickets.

It is very enjoyable traveling by sea.

Notes

1. convenient *adj.* 方便的，便利的
2. economical *adj.* 经济的，实惠的
3. luxurious *adj.* 奢侈的，豪华的
4. comparatively *adv.* 相对来说
5. appointed *adj.* 指定的

Passage Two

Sample Itinerary of 10 Days' China Highlight Tour

Day 1   Arrive in Shanghai from Hong Kong by plane.

Day 2   Sightsee in Shanghai (the Yu Yuan Garden and the Jade Buddha Temple).

Day 3   Fly to Beijing in the morning and sightsee in the afternoon (Tian'anmen Square). Watch a performance of Beijing Opera in the evening.

Day 4   Sightsee in Beijing (the Great Wall and the Ming Tombs).

Day 5   Sightsee in Beijing (the Summer Palace, the Temple of Heaven and the Palace Museum).

Day 6   Fly to Xi'an in the morning and sightsee in Xi'an in the afternoon (the Great Wild Goose Pagoda, the Forest of Steles and the Old City Wall).

Day 7   Sightsee in Xi'an (the Terra-cotta Warriors, the Huaqing Pool Hot Spring

and the Ban Po Ruins).

Day 8   Fly to Guilin in the morning and sightsee in Guilin in the afternoon (Piled Festoon Hill, Seven Star Cave).

Day 9   Boat trip along the Lijiang River.

Day 10   Fly to Guangzhou in the morning and leave for Hong Kong.

Notes

1. itinerary   *n.* 路线，线路
2. highlight   *n.* 亮点，精彩的部分
3. warrior   *n.* 武士，战士
4. ruin   *n.* 废墟，遗迹

Part Ⅴ   Skill Training

Ⅰ. Matches.

a. specific   1. 缆车

b. warrior   2. 代理处

c. ski   3. 阳光

d. appointed   4. 厌倦的

e. agency   5. 出发

f. cable cars   6. 滑雪

g. luxurious   7. 武士，战士

h. bored   8. 指定的

i. depart   9. 奢侈的，豪华的

j. sunshine   10. 具体的，确切的，明确的

Ⅱ. Choices.

| details | extra | work out | agency | as | business | course |
| about | easiest | in | | | | |

The ___1___ way to help you plan your travel is to go to a travel ___2___ for help. There

you can inquire ___3___ where to go and how to go. You can also ask various questions a-
bout the ___4___ such ___5___ how far away the city is, whether the bus or train goes there,
what kind of hotels you can stay in. Of ___6___ you won't miss the information about the
details of the places of the interest there and what not. ___7___ fact you simply give all the
details you can and let them ___8___ the best possible plan for you. This is their ___9___ and
they can do it better and even more economically than you can and there is no ___10___ cost
to you.

Ⅲ. Translate the following sentences into Chinese.

1. If your friends have been there, you can talk to them.

2. The suggestions all from their own experience are very useful.

3. They may give you detailed and vivid descriptions about the place.

4. For example, which part is more interesting than others, how can you enjoy
yourself better, or what should you pay more attention to.

5. Most important at all, they can offer some valuable advice for the trip.

Ⅳ. Translate the following sentences into English.

1. 有好几种方法可以提前了解你希望去观光的国家和地区。

2. 有经验的旅行社会为你提供许多信息。

3. 最重要的是，他们随时愿意帮助你。

4. 除此之外，你还可以阅读旅游书籍或者浏览旅游网站。

5. 它们也很有用，有时甚至胜过朋友或旅行社，因为只要你需要，任何时候想看
都可以。

Ⅴ. Read through the dialogue and finish the following exercises.

(Miss Bush is talking to a travel agent in London.)

(A＝the travel agent   B＝Miss Bush)

A：Can I help you?

B：I'm intending to go to a conference in Sydney for three weeks.

A：Do you want the excursion fare or the full return fare?

B：Can I get a stopover on an excursion fare?

A：Of course, if you pay the full return fare, then you can have unlimited stop-
overs.

B：The thing is that I've got two weeks' holiday after the conference and I've never

been out that way before at all to Australia or the Far East. Where exactly can I go?

A: There're Singapore, Teheran, Kuwait, Athens. You've really got quite a lot of choices you know.

B: Well, it sounds marvelous.

A: Well, it's once in a lifetime, you know. I've never been.

B: The thing is, actually, that I'm absolutely terrified of flying. I'm hoping I can persuade my two friends, who are also going to the conference, to stop over with me on the way back. By the way, one of them is in Cairo at the moment. Would it be possible for me to stop over there on my way to Sydney?

A: There are plenty of flights to Cairo and then plenty more onwards from Cairo to Sydney.

B: The thing is, I think I'd better go and persuade Mr. Adams that, you know, he'd like to stop with me in Cairo...go and discuss with him and then come back to you in a day or two, if that's all right.

A: Well, it's OK.

1. Choose the best answers.

(1) Miss Bush comes to the travel agency to _____.

A. ask for some information

B. buy a ticket

C. talk to a friend

(2) Miss Bush's main purpose of the trip is _____.

A. sightseeing in Australia and the Far East

B. visiting a friend in Cairo

C. attending a conference in Sydney

(3) Miss Bush will probably buy _____.

A. an excursion fare

B. a full return fare

C. a single ticket

(4) Miss Bush's trip will probably be _____.

A. London—Sydney—Cairo

B. London—Kuwait—Sydney

C. London—Cairo—Sydney

(5) Miss Bush will probably come to the travel agency again _____.

A. the day after tomorrow

B. next week

C. in two weeks

2. Decide whether the statements are true(T) or false(F).

(1) Though Miss Bush is used to traveling by air, she's still frightened this time. (   )

(2) Miss Bush's conference in Sydney will last for three weeks. (   )

(3) Miss Bush thinks that the full return fare is better than the excursion fare because she can have a stopover. (   )

(4) Miss Bush wants to visit not only Australia but also the Far East this time. (   )

(5) Though Miss Bush thinks that the full return ticket is quite expensive, she will accept that because it is once in a lifetime. (   )

Part Ⅵ   Knowledge Expansion

如何挑选旅行社

旅客报名时，可以要求旅行社出示旅游管理部门颁发的《旅行社业务经营许可证》和工商行政管理部门颁发的营业执照。如报名点与旅行社总部在一处办公，可要求提供证照原件；如报名点远离旅行社总部，应要求其提供旅行社总部的办公地址和联系电话，以备核实。参加旅行社组织的出境游，应当要求旅行社提供经旅游管理部门批准的证书。如果参加的是无证非法经营的"野马社"，旅客的权益将很难得到保障。

需要提醒的是，不能单凭旅行社报价高低来取舍。一般来说，旅行社的报价有两种：一种是全包价，即包括交通、住宿、餐饮、门票等；另一种是小包价，即只包一部分费用或某一段行程中的费用。因此，旅客在报名时，不要谁的价格便宜就跟谁走，一定要问清楚旅行社的报价中包括哪些部分，还有哪些费用需要自理。有一些不正规的旅行社，为了争抢客源而拼命压低报价，旅客对此须格外注意。旅客要把旅行社的各种口头承诺以书面形式予以确定，并写入旅游合同。

此外，出境游尤须注意提防旅行社"耍花样"。一段时间以来，出境游巨大的利润空间令众多旅行社趋之若鹜，各种问题也随之产生。一些没有出境游合法资质的旅行社非法承接业务，采取层层转包的方式非法牟利，骗取旅客的钱财。此外，无证导游诱骗旅客购买伪劣商品，旅游时间、旅游景点"缩水"，交通工具、住宿条件达不到约定标准，饮食卫生条件无法保证等情况，也时有发生。

在境外购物时，旅客应注意辨别商品真伪和质量，择优购买并保存好商品质量保

证书及发票。出境游的旅客应及时投保。根据有关规定，旅行社目前购买的是"旅游责任险"。旅客也可以选择购买"个人旅游意外险"。

如果在境外旅游过程中与旅行社发生纠纷，旅客应冷静处理，先随旅游团出入境，避免发生非法滞留，同时应保留所有相关的消费凭证，以便回国后向消费者协会等机构投诉。

Chapter 3

Staying in a Hotel

Part I Lead-in

【本章简介】

住宿是旅游的六大主要环节之一。本章以酒店住宿中的各个不同情景为主线，围绕真实工作任务设置不同场景，突出行业工作语言功能。本章选取了酒店预订、登记入住、行李接送、引入房间、整理房间、洗衣服务等数个真实情景，既有大型高星级酒店的最新工作模式，又不脱离酒店业的核心工作轨迹，其涉及的工作流程和理念适合各种类型的酒店企业。在教学素材的形式方面，突显酒店业以人为本的特征，以口头交际为主，强调会话沟通能力，以及对服务过程与服务内容表达能力的培养。

【教学目标】

1. 掌握与酒店服务相关的专业词汇及常用表达；
2. 熟悉酒店业的核心工作轨迹及服务流程；
3. 培养酒店服务一线工作场景中的沟通会话及表达能力；
4. 掌握酒店员工的基本礼仪和素质要求。

【背景知识】

1. Hotel Types

inn	旅馆，饭店	hotel	饭店，酒店
lodge	小饭店	motel	汽车旅馆
hostel	招待所	budget hotel	廉价旅馆

2. Star-rated Hotels

economy hotel（one-star hotel）　一星级饭店

some comfort hotel（two-star hotel）　二星级饭店

average hotel（three-star hotel）　三星级饭店

high comfort hotel（four-star hotel）　四星级饭店

deluxe hotel（five-star hotel）　五星级饭店

Part II Situational Dialogues

Dialogue One

Group Reservation

(R＝receptionist   G＝guest)

R：Good morning, Guangzhou Hotel. Reservation Desk. May I help you?

G：Yes, our company will hold an exhibition in your city, so I'd like to make a reservation for my group.

R：What kind of rooms do you prefer, sir?

G：I'd like to have twin rooms.

R：May I have your name and nationality, sir?

G：Samuel Anderson from the US.

R：For which dates, Mr. Anderson?

G：From January 20 to 26.

R：How many guests will be there in your party?

G：We'll have 20 people altogether.

R：That'll be 10 twin rooms, right?

G：Yes, that's right.

R：OK, 10 double rooms from January 20 to 26. Wait a minute please. Let me have a check. Yes, we still have those rooms available.

G：Good. How much do you charge?

R：A twin room in our hotel is 1,200 yuan RMB per night. And we offer a 15 percent discount for group reservation. So, that'll be only 1,020 yuan RMB.

G：Sounds great. I'll have them.

R：Do you prefer front view or rear view?

G：We'd like to have rooms with rear view, which will be much quieter.

R：OK, I'll confirm your information. 10 twin rooms with rear view for Samuel Anderson, from January 20 to 26. Am I right?

G：Yes, that's right. One more thing, do you have sports facilities and swimming pool?

R: Yes, we do. We have a standard-sized swimming pool in our hotel, which are open 24 hours a day. We also have a fitness center with all sets of sports facilities.

G: How much do you charge?

R: They are all free for our staying guests.

G: That'll be great. Could you meet us at the airport?

R: Yes, sir. After you have booked air tickets, please call and tell us your flight number. We'll pick you up on time.

G: That's really kind of you.

R: It's my pleasure. Is there anything else I can do for you?

G: That's all. Thanks a lot.

R: You're welcome. We are looking forward to your coming.

Notes

1. nationality   *n.* 国籍
2. front view or rear view   临街的还是不临街的
3. sports facilities   运动设施
4. standard-sized   *adj.* 标准尺寸的
5. fitness center   健身中心
6. charge 有多种用法。作名词时，表示费用、价钱、代价、控诉、谴责、管理、照顾。例如：There is no charge of admission.（免费入场。）作动词时，表示收费、索价、记账、控诉、装载、充电、赊购。例如：Please charge the money to my account.（请把这些钱记在我的账上。）

Dialogue Two

Cleaning-up Service

(A＝attendant   G＝guest)

A: Housekeeping. May I come in?

G: Come in, please.

A: Good afternoon, Mr. Burne Jones. Is it the proper time for me to clean your room now?

G: I've just taken a shower, and it's quite a mess in the bathroom. Would you mind cleaning it a little?

A: Of course not. I'll clean it up right away.

(The room attendant finished it several minutes later.)

A: May I remove the files on your desk so that I can dust it?

G: Just do it. Can I have some more juice in the mini-bar?

A: OK. I'll send it up later.

(After cleaning up the room.)

A: Is there anything else I can do for you?

G: Oh, yes. Can you bring me a hair-dryer when you come back?

A: Sure. I'll be back later.

(A few minutes later.)

A: Here is the hair-dryer and juice, sir. I'll put the juice in your mini-bar. Please enjoy it.

G: Thank you very much. You're so helpful.

A: It's my pleasure. According to the weather forecast, it'll rain tonight. Please don't forget to close the window before you go to bed.

G: Thank you so much. I haven't got any information about weather condition.

A: You're welcome. Have a nice evening.

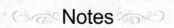

Notes

1. dust   *v.* 擦去……的灰尘

2. hair-dryer   *n.* 吹风机

3. mini-bar   *n.* 小冰箱

4. weather forecast   天气预报

**Dialogue Three**

Laundry Service

(R＝receptionist   A＝attendant   G＝guest)

R: Good morning. This is Front Office. What can I do for you?

G: Good morning. I wonder if you offer laundry service.

R: Yes, we do. We have different services such as washing, dry-cleaning, ironing and mending.

G: That's great. Could you tell me the laundry service hour?

R: Sure. If your laundry is picked up before 10 a. m. , it'll be returned to your room by 8 p. m. on the same day. If it is picked up before 4 p. m. , it will be returned by 12 a. m. the next day.

G: How do you charge it?

R: The laundry rate is in the stationery folder on the table, sir.

G: Do you offer express service?

R: Yes, if you are in a hurry, we can deliver your laundry within 4 hours at a 50% extra charge.

G: OK, I see. I have some clothes to be cleaned. Could you send someone to Room 1203 to pick them up?

R: Certainly, sir. The room attendant will be in your room in a minute.

(A knock at the door.)

A: Laundry service. May I come in?

G: Come in, please.

A: Good morning, sir. I'm here to pick your laundry.

G: I want this three-piece suit to be dry cleaned and pressed.

A: OK. Would you please fill out the laundry list and mark them down?

G: Here it goes. What about the silk dress? I'm afraid it will be wrinkled in dry cleaning.

A: The silk dress should be washed by hand in cold water. Otherwise, the color will fade.

G: Thank you for your reminding. I'll mark them down. Well, there is a stain on this shirt. I'd like it to be removed before washing.

A: What kind of stain is it, sir?

G: I spilled some sauce on it in dinner. I don't hope the shirt will be ruined.

A: We'll try our best to remove it. Anything else can I do for you?

G: That's all. When can I get them back?

A: We'll deliver your laundry back to your room before 8 this evening.

G: Thank you.

A: You're welcome.

Notes

1. laundry   *n.* 洗衣店，洗衣房；待洗的衣物；洗好的衣物；洗熨
2. stationery folder   文件夹
3. press   *v.* 熨烫
4. stain   *n.* 污点；色斑

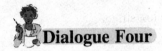

Dialogue Four

Check Out

(R＝receptionist   G＝guest)

R：Good morning, Mr. Hill. May I help you?

G：Yes, I'd like to check out.

R：May I have your room key?

G：Here you are.

R：How was everything?

G：The hotel environment is great. The beds are really comfortable, and the foods are wonderful. We especially like the Chinese food in your restaurant.

R：I'm glad you enjoyed your staying.

G：You can count on it.

R：Mr. Hill, this is your bill. A single room for three nights, 180 yuan per night, that comes to 540 yuan. Also you have meals in the restaurant, which comes to 80 yuan. So, that makes a total of 620 yuan altogether.

G：OK. Let me have a look. That's right.

R：How will you make payment? By cash or by credit card?

G：I'll pay by credit card. Here you are.

R：Please sign your name here.

G：OK, done.

R：This is your invoice. Please take good care of it. I'll call the bellboy to help you with your luggage.

G：That'll be very helpful. Thank you.

R：You're welcome. We're looking forward to seeing you next time.

∾ Notes ∾

1. make payment   付款
2. credit card   信用卡
3. invoice   发票

| Part Ⅲ   Vocabulary & Useful Expressions

Ⅰ. Useful Words

1. Ways of Reservation

telephone reservation	fax reservation
reservation on Internet	mail reservation
oral reservation	contract reservation

2. The Necessary Information in Room Reservation

name	telephone number
room types	amounts of rooms
number of guests	nationality
date/time of arrival	date/time of departure
discount and payment	length of staying

3. Room Types in a Hotel

single room   单人房（一张单人床）

twin room   双人对床房（两张单人床）

double room   双人房（一张双人床）

big single room   大床房（一张双人大床）

triple room   三人房（三张单人床）

economy room 经济间	standard room 标准间
standard suite 标准套房	junior suite 普通套房
business suite 商务套房	duplex suite 复式套房

deluxe suite　豪华套房　　　　　　　　presidential suite　总统套房

4. Items of Clothes

T-shirt　T恤　　　　　　　　　　　　　shorts　短裤

underwear　内衣　　　　　　　　　　　　underpants　内裤

brassiere　胸衣　　　　　　　　　　　　blouse　（女）衬衫

dress　女装，连衣裙　　　　　　　　　　skirt　裙子

tie　领带　　　　　　　　　　　　　　　scarf　围巾

stockings　长筒袜　　　　　　　　　　　socks　短袜

5. Words Related to Laundry Service

dry-cleaning recommended　最好干洗　　　dry cleaning　干洗

washing　水洗　　　　　　　　　　　　　machine washable　可机洗

Do not wash　不可水洗　　　　　　　　　hand wash　手洗

cold wash　冷水洗　　　　　　　　　　　warm wash　温水洗

Do not wring　不可拧干　　　　　　　　　Do not spin　不可脱水

Do not soak　不可浸泡　　　　　　　　　bleaching　漂白

No bleach　不可漂白　　　　　　　　　　drip dry　滴干

line dry　挂干　　　　　　　　　　　　　tumble dry　烘干

iron and pressing　熨烫　　　　　　　　　cold iron　低温熨烫

hot iron　热熨烫　　　　　　　　　　　　steam iron　蒸汽熨烫

iron on wrong side　反面熨烫

Ⅱ. Useful Expressions

1. May I help you? / What can I do for you?

   有什么需要帮忙的吗？

2. May I have your name and phone number, please?

   请问您的姓名和电话。

3. In whose name is the reservation made?

   请问是以谁的名义预订的呢？

4. What kind of room would you like?

   您想要哪种类型的房间？

5. For which date? /For when?

要预订哪一天?

6. I'd like to book a room, please.

我想预订一个房间。

7. What time will you be arriving? / When will you arrive?

请问您几点到达?

8. I'm sorry, but we're fully booked for those days.

不好意思,我们那几天的预订已满。

9. Sorry, we're overbooked. But I can recommend you another hotel.

对不起,我们的预订已满,不过我可以向您推荐另一家酒店。

10. Do you prefer a front view or a rear view?

您想要朝街房还是背街房?

11. Can you keep the suite blocked for Mr. Hans?

您能为汉斯先生保留这间套房吗?

12. We are looking forward to seeing you next Sunday.

期待下周日您的到来。

13. I'm always at your service.

随时乐意为您服务。

14. Would you like to check in, sir?

您要入住酒店吗?

15. I'd like to check in.

我想登记入住。

16. Do you have a reservation?

请问您有预订吗?

17. Would you please fill in this registration form?

请填写一下入住登记表好吗?

18. May I see your passport, please?

请出示您的护照。

19. Could you please sign here?

请在此处签名。

20. The bellman will show you up to your room.

行李员会带您到房间。

21. Our check-in time is 2 o'clock in the afternoon. Would you mind waiting until then?

我们入住登记的时间是下午 2 点,请您等一下好吗?

22. I have made a reservation in the name of George Smith.

我以乔治·史密斯的名义预订了一个房间。

23. Do you have any rooms available? / Do you have any vacancies?

有空房间吗？

24. Can you give me a wake-up call in the morning?

您能早上叫醒我吗？

25. Can you tell the room maid not to clean the room in the morning? I want to sleep late.

能否告诉客房服务员不要在早上打扫房间？我想睡个懒觉。

26. Wish you a pleasant stay.

祝您在酒店住得愉快。

27. What time would you like us to clean your room?

您希望我们什么时候为您打扫房间呢？

28. The pillowcases are dirty. Could you change them for me?

枕套脏了，请换一下好吗？

29. If you are in a hurry, we have a two-hour express laundry service.

如果您着急，我们有2小时的加急洗衣服务。

30. We can deliver your laundry within 4 hours at a 50% extra charge. / We can deliver your laundry within 4 hours, but we charge 50% more.

我们可以在4小时内送回您的送洗衣物，但要加收50%的额外费用。

31. We have different services such as washing, dry-cleaning, ironing and mending.

我们提供不同种类的服务，如水洗、干洗、熨烫和缝补。

32. I would like to store my laptop in one of your safe-deposit boxes.

我想把我的笔记本电脑存放在酒店的保险柜里。

33. Could you get a repairman to fix the window?

能派人来修理一下窗户吗？

34. The bath tub in Room 2135 is out of order/service. Could you please send someone to repair/fix it?

2135房间的浴缸坏了，请派人来修理一下好吗？

35. The water tap was dripping all night long.

水龙头一晚上都在滴水。

36. I would like to have an adaptor. / I need an adaptor.

我想要一个转换插头。

37. This is Room 1105. Can you send me an iron, please?

这是 1105 房间。请送一个电熨斗。

38. The TV set in my room doesn't give clear pictures.

我房间的电视图像不清楚。

39. Please accept my apology on behalf of the hotel.

请接受我代表酒店向您道歉。

40. We have free Internet service. / You can use Internet in the room for free.

在房间上网是免费的。

41. The room enjoys the ocean/sea view.

这个房间是海景房。

42. This is your room key. Our bellboy will show you to your room.

这是您房间的钥匙。我们的行李员会带您去房间。

43. The hotel provides free shoe shining service for its guests.

酒店为客人提供免费的擦鞋服务。

44. What's the rate of this service?

这项服务怎么收费？

45. The baby-sitting service charges 20 yuan per hour, with a minimum of 4 hours.

托儿服务每小时收费 20 元，最低从 4 小时开始计费。

46. Here are three kinds of medicines for stomachache. Would you like me to read the instructions to you?

这里有三种治疗胃痛的药，需要我给您读一下说明吗？

47. Good evening. May I do the turn-down service for you now?

晚上好。现在可以为您开夜床吗？

48. May I vacuum the blanket for you now?

我现在可以为地毯吸尘吗？

49. When would you like me to turn on the lights (for you)?

什么时候能为您把灯打开？

50. I just had a bath and it is a mess in the bathroom. Could you clean the bathroom a little?

我刚洗过澡，浴室里乱糟糟的，你能稍微收拾一下浴室吗？

Part IV   Reading Materials

Passage One

Front Office Organizational Structure

The front desk of a hotel is perhaps the most important area of the organization. The employees that make up this department are the first and sometimes only representatives of the establishment with whom guests interact. Although the organizational structure of the hotel's front office varies depending upon whether the facility is a small business or a large resort, certain roles are found within all organizations.

Front Desk Manager

The front desk manager or front desk supervisor oversees all front office operations for the hotel. As a staff manager, this individual schedules employees to ensure that there is proper coverage at all times. She also implements any policies or procedures that are administered by hotel management. When VIPs, such as celebrities or dignitaries, stay at the establishment, she is often responsible for giving them the personal attention they require. In most instances, the front desk manager reports to the hotel's general manager.

Reservations

The reception and reservation employees of a hotel front office interact with guests the most. Reservation clerks communicate with the perspective guests via the telephone and Internet, scheduling their stays and documenting any special needs they may have. For example, if a guest requests a room on a nonsmoking floor, the reservation clerk will make special note of this, so that an appropriate room will be ready when the guest arrives.

Reception

When guests arrive, front desk clerks check them in, inputing their names into the facilities registry, assigning them to a room and answering any basic questions or requests the guests may have throughout their stay. For example, a guest may call the front desk to report a leaky bathroom faucet. The clerk would then contact the maintenance department so that the appropriate repairs can be made. At the end of the guests' stay, a front desk clerk checks them out. In addition, the clerk reports any concerns the guest may have to the management.

Porter Service

A hotel bellhop or porter greets guests once they checked into the establishment. This individual carries the guests' luggage while showing them to their room. Ensuring that everything in the room is in order and properly working, the porter checks room equipment, such as lighting and ventilation. He may also instruct visitors in the operation of hotel systems, such as the television remote control and telephones.

Concierge

The concierge of a hotel is a front office professional who coordinates guests' entertainments, travel and other activities. Any time guests have a question, such as directions to local attractions, she finds the answer as quickly as possible. In addition, she makes restaurant reservations, orders car service and may even arrange personal shopping for the guests.

∽ Notes ∼

1. employee   *n.* 雇员，职员，员工

2. representative   *n.* 代表，代理人   *adj.* 有代表性的，典型的

3. establishment   *n.* 企业，大型机关，旅馆；建立

4. interact   *v.* 相互作用（影响），互相配合；交流，沟通

5. vary   *v.* 呈现不同，变化，改变

6. resort   *n.* 度假胜地，旅游胜地

7. supervisor   *n.* 监督者，管理者，主管人

8. oversee   *v.* 监督，监视

9. individual   *adj.* 单独的，个人的   *n.* 个人，人，某一类型的人

10. schedule   *v.* 排定，安排，列入   *n.* 时间表，日常安排

11. coverage   *n.* 新闻报道；提供的数量；覆盖范围

12. implement   *v.* 实习，完成，执行   *n.* 工具，器具

13. policy   *n.* 政策，方针；计谋，方法

14. procedure   *n.* 程序，过程，步骤；手续

15. administer   *v.* 管理，支配

16. celebrity   *n.* （尤指娱乐界的）名人，名流

17. dignitary   *n.* 显要人物，权贵

18. perspective   *n.* 远景，前途，希望；观点，想法   *adj.* 透视的

19. document   *v.* 用文件证明，为……提供文档   *n.* 公文，文件，证书

20. appropriate   *adj.* 合适的，恰当的

21. registry   *n.* 档案室，登记簿存放处；注册处；挂号处

22. leaky   *adj.* 有漏洞的，渗漏的

23. faucet   *n.* 水龙头，旋塞

24. bellhop   *n.* 信差；做杂役的男侍者

25. ventilation   *n.* 空气流通，通风设备

26. instruct   *v.* 命令，指示，吩咐，通知

27. concierge   *n.* 看门人，门房；礼宾部经理

28. coordinate   *v.* 使协调，使调和；搭配   *adj.* 同等的，同样重要的

29. entertainment   *n.* 款待，请客；娱乐活动，供消遣的东西

30. attraction   *n.* 吸引力，具有吸引力的事物

Passage Two

The Housekeeping Department in a Hotel

As one of the most integral departments within the hotel, the housekeeping department is responsible for the immaculate care and upkeep of all guest rooms and public spaces. The laundry and valet service and many personal services are also parts of their jobs. In a competitive hotel market, it is service and cleanliness that really make an impact on your guests and determine whether they will return.

The housekeeping department is headed by the executive housekeeper and its staff includes housemaids, housemen (room boys), floor clerks, linen room attendant and seamstresses. Such housekeeping staff as floor clerks, housemaids and room boys all have direct contact with the guest and contribute to the guests' overall experience with the hotel.

The job of a housemaid or houseman is especially important, for a comfortable, clean, quiet and well-appointed room with a large soft bed is what every traveler looks for at the end of his or her journey or a day's sightseeing. Well, an unclean waste basket or bath tub, or not completely dried bad sheet can upset a tired guest and lead to a bad impression on the hotel.

This department is required to make the guests' stay comfortable and pleasing. Any reasonable request must be fulfilled. But good service means more than fulfilling requests. The staff should offer to do more for the guests.

As a room attendant, your main duties would include:
- Introducing room facilities;
- Making up rooms;
- Making or changing beds;
- Dusting furniture;
- Cleaning floors and carpets;
- Washing bathrooms;
- Replacing towels;
- Offering laundry service;
- Doing turn-down service.

Room attendants also offer other personal services to satisfy guests' needs, such as wake-up service, shoeshine service and baby-sitting. Whenever and wherever possible, the staff should offer to meet guests' personal requirements. Finally, to be competent hotel staff, they should be capable of handling with unexpected emergency and try to minimize the damage of negative influence.

Notes

1. integral *adj.* 构成整体所必需的；不可或缺的

2. immaculate *adj.* 整洁的，无污迹的；精确的

3. upkeep *n.* 保养，维持

4. valet *n.* 贴身仆人，仆从；（饭店中）为顾客停车的服务员

5. impact *n. &v.* 影响，作用

6. executive *n.* 经理，管理人员；行政领导；决策人

7. housemaid *n.* 女佣，女仆；客房服务员

8. linen *n.* 亚麻布；家庭日用织品

9. seamstress *n.* 女裁缝，做针线活的妇女

10. contribute *v.* 捐献，捐助；是……的原因之一

11. fulfill *v.* 履行，完成，实现

12. turn-down service 做晚床服务

13. shoeshine *n.* 鞋油；擦皮鞋

14. baby-sit *v.* 当临时保姆，照看孩子

15. capable *adj.* 有能力的，有技能的，足以胜任的

16. emergency *n.* 紧急情况，突发事件

| Part Ⅴ   **Skill Training**

Ⅰ. Matches.

a.	business hotel	1.	青年旅馆
b.	luxury hotel	2.	温泉酒店
c.	resort hotel	3.	招待所
d.	small，family-run hotel	4.	机场酒店
e.	motel	5.	度假酒店/度假村
f.	sports hotel	6.	乡村旅店
g.	conference hotel	7.	体育酒店
h.	country house hotel	8.	汽车旅馆
i.	airport hotel	9.	家庭旅馆
j.	guest house	10.	豪华酒店
k.	youth hostel	11.	会议酒店
l.	spa hotel	12.	商务酒店

Ⅱ. Translate the following sentences into Chinese.

1. May I remove the things on your desk so that I can dust it?

2. Can I have some more juice for the mini-bar?

3. Do you prefer your laundry by express service or to be returned on the same day?

4. The indemnity shall not exceed ten times of the laundry charge.

5. It takes time to repair the air-conditioner in your room. I'm afraid you have to change to another room.

Ⅲ. Translate the following sentences into English.

1. 我向您保证，这类事情以后不会再发生了。

2. 如果您有问题，请随时找我们。

3. 希望您在我们饭店的这段时间生活愉快！

4. 这里是失物招领处，我们找到了您的手机。

5. 我和我丈夫今晚要出去，你能帮助照看一下我们的孩子吗？

Ⅳ. Situational play.

Situation 1

You are a front office receptionist of a hotel. A guest comes to you for information about your hotel. Make a dialogue with your partner, using the following key words:

1. conference room	6. tennis courts
2. suite bathroom	7. swimming pool
3. laundry service	8. beauty salon
4. Wi-Fi access	9. fitness center
5. air conditioning	

Situation 2

A travel agent makes a group reservation in your hotel through telephone. Make a dialogue with your partner.

Part Ⅵ   Knowledge Expansion

Ⅰ. 语言指南

1. Hotel keeping is known as the "hospitality industry" (殷勤行业) or "courtesy industry" (礼貌行业) or "service industry". Our aim is to create a "home away from home" for all our guests. We believe in old-fashioned good manners and politeness. Practice these till they become second nature—till you are courteous automatically.

2. Always remember to practice traditional Chinese hospitality.

3. Give guests your best in service and in kind.

4. Let them have quietness and privacy—unobtrusive service.

5. Anticipate their needs—don't wait for them to ask.

6. Give way to them (stand aside and let them go first).

7. Always remember to look for "cues" in the environment (察言观色) when deal-

ing with guests—those little hints to tell us if they are happy, satisfied, comfortable. This will help us to avoid making them discontented and angry. Before the point is reached when guests complain, we should notice their dissatisfaction:

● tightened facial expressions;

● impatient movements of fingers or feet;

● a sharp tone or voice.

When these "cues" appear, we should immediately apologize, and put things right.

8. Different cultures have different sets of etiquette and acceptable ways of behaving.

e. g. Westerners do not think it's rude to contradict or disagree. While to many people in China, this is not acceptable.

9. In China, however, we often laugh to hide our ignorance or when embarrassed. Westerners may think you are laughing at them.

10. Good manners mean you never knowingly upset anyone.

11. Honesty is the best policy.

Ⅱ. 知识链接

Burj Al-Arab—Ultimate Luxury

The Burj Al-Arab in Dubai is the world's tallest hotel building. At 321 meters, it is taller than the Eiffel Tower and only 60 meters shorter than the Empire State Building in New York. This unique sail-shaped building stands on an artificial island in the Persian Gulf. The hotel lobby is big enough for a 38-storey to fit inside it.

The Burj Al-Arab does not have ordinary bedrooms—instead, it has 202 suites. The price for a night's stay in the least expensive suite is over ¥10,000. Every suite has a spectacular sea view. Rolls Royce limousines pick up the hotel's guests from Dubai International Airport, 25 kilometers away. Alternatively, you can land your helicopter on the helipad high up on the side of the hotel.

The most luxurious suites are the two royal suites on the 25 th floor. They both have a private elevator, a private cinema, rotating beds, and even dressing rooms which are larger than the average hotel bedroom. A night in one of those suites can cost over ¥150,000.

Diners at the Burj Al-Arab are spoilt for choice: they can dine 200 meters above the sea in the Al Muntaha restaurant, below the waves in the famous Al Mahara seafood restaurant, which has an underwater entrance, or alfresco on the beach. In total there are eight bars and restaurants in the hotel.

Although the Burj Al-Arab is one of the world's most expensive hotels, it will probably never make a profit.

Notes

1. Burj Al-Arab（伯瓷酒店，又称阿拉伯之塔酒店、迪拜帆船酒店）：a luxury hotel located in Dubai，which is also known as Tower of the Arabs（阿拉伯之塔）. It stands on an artificial island and is connected to the mainland by a private curving bridge. It is an iconic structure，designed to symbolize Dubai's urban transformation and to mimic the sail of a boat.

2. Dubai（迪拜）：a state on the Arabian Gulf，part of the United Arab Emirates.

3. Empire State Building（帝国大厦）：a famous landmark in New York City.

4. Persian Gulf（波斯湾）：a shallow arm of the Arabian Sea between Iran and the Arabian peninsula，the oil fields of which are among the most productive in the world.

5. Rolls Royce（劳斯莱斯）：a very expensive and comfortable car made by a British company.

Chapter 4

Food and Beverage

Part I Lead-in

【本章简介】

本章主要介绍旅游服务过程中重要的一个环节——餐饮服务。餐饮服务主要表现为就餐前的相应预订工作，以及根据中西方餐饮的不同文化风俗（如中国对各种烹饪菜肴的偏爱，西方对餐桌礼仪的要求），恰当得体地点餐、就餐。读者通过情景对话以及延伸阅读等了解导游在游客就餐过程中应起的作用，最后通过练习进一步了解并掌握导游业务方面的知识。

【教学目标】

1. 掌握与餐饮服务相关的专业词汇及用语；
2. 熟悉相应的就餐流程，并能够用英语熟练地表达；
3. 了解中国的主要菜系特点及知名菜肴；
4. 能够引导游客以得体的方式吃西餐。

【背景知识】

俗话说"民以食为天"，可见餐饮在整个旅游过程中的作用非常重要，饮食的好坏将直接影响到旅游的正常行程以及游客对旅行社的信任。不同地域因食品原料、烹饪方法、饮食习惯等的不同，形成了丰富多彩的饮食文化。作为导游，应尽量依据不同游客的口味，推荐适合个人的菜肴，满足游客的不同需求。同时，要注意体弱多病游客的饮食禁忌，如对海鲜过敏、不能饮酒等，避免游客在旅游途中生病，耽误行程。

Part II Situational Dialogues

Dialogue One

(Betty is making a phone call to Sunny Holiday Restaurant to make a reservation

for a party of ten.)

（R＝reservationist   B＝Betty）

R：Good morning. Sunny Holiday Restaurant. May I help you?

B：Yes, I'd like to reserve a table for this Saturday night, please.

R：Certainly, Miss. For how many people?

B：Let me see. Ten people.

R：And what time should we expect you?

B：At 6：30.

R：Would you like a table in the main restaurant or in a private room?

B：A private room, please.

R：Yes, Miss, but the minimum charge for a private room is 1,000 yuan.

B：OK, no problem.

R：May I have your name and telephone number, please?

B：It is Betty Green and my number is 65765321.

R：So it is a table for 10 at 6：30 under the name of Betty Green.

B：That's right. By the way, could you fax the menu with the name of the private room? My fax number is 65765222.

R：Yes, 65765222. We'll be sure to fax you the menu with the name of the private room as soon as possible. Is there anything I can do for you, Miss Green?

B：No, thanks.

R：OK. By the way, we can only keep your table till 7：00 p. m. , since that will be a peak season.

B：OK, I see.

R：Thank you. We are looking forward to seeing you this Saturday evening.

B：Good-bye.

❧ Notes ❧

1. Would you like a table in the main restaurant or in a private room?   您想订在大厅还是在包间呢?

2. the minimum charge for a private room   包间的最低消费

3. By the way, could you fax the menu with the name of the private room?   顺便问一下，能否将包间的名字和菜单一起传真过来?

4. By the way, we can only keep your private room till 7：00 p. m. , since that will

be a peak season. 顺便说一下，您预订的包间只能预留到晚上 7 点，因为那
段时间是（用餐）高峰期。

Dialogue Two

(John and his friends go to a restaurant to have dinner and a head waiter is helping them to find a table.)

(H＝head waiter   J＝John)

H：Good evening, sir. Welcome to our restaurant. Do you have a reservation，sir?

J：I'm afraid we haven't reserved it. Do you have a table for four?

H：Let me see. We have a table in the smoking section，if that is OK.

J：I can't stand the smell of that. Do you have any other table for us?

H：I'm sorry, we haven't got any other vacant table at present. Would you please wait in the lounge for about five minutes? I'll seat you as soon as the table is available.

J：All right. Thank you.

(Five minutes later.)

H：I am sorry to have kept you waiting, sir. Now we have a table for you. Would you step this way, please?

J：(John suddenly catches sight of a table near the window.) May we sit at the table by the window?

H：Sorry, that table has been reserved.

J：It's a pity.

H：Well, that table in the corner is quite good. It's near the band platform. There will be a performance during the meal time. You could enjoy it comfortably.

J：OK, we'll take it.

H：Now, this is your table. It's No. 14 and the waiter will be with you right a-way.

J：Thank you very much.

Notes

1. I'm sorry, we haven't got any other vacant table at present.   对不起，我们目前没有其他空余的餐桌。

2. Would you please wait in the lounge for about five minutes?　请在休息室等大概 5 分钟好吗？

3. I'll seat you as soon as the table is available.　只要有空余的餐桌我就安排你们入座。

4. It's near the band platform. There will be a performance during the meal time. （您的餐桌）靠近乐队表演区，在进餐时会有演出。

Dialogue Three

(Mary and her friends want to have some Chinese food for their dinner. The waiter tries to recommend some dishes and takes her order.)

(W＝waiter　　M＝Mary)

W：Good evening, Madam. May I have your order now?

M：Let me see your menu.

W：Here you are.

M：This is our first time in a Chinese restaurant and we know nothing about Chinese dishes. Would you recommend some traditional Chinese food for us?

W：OK. We have a wide variety of traditional Chinese food and wine for you to choose from in our restaurant. According to our Chinese way, people always have cold dishes and drinks first, then hot dishes and rice, soup or tea is the last course. For cold dishes, I recommend you to order Plain Boiled Chicken and Mushroom with Duck Webs.

M：That sounds great! We'll take them. But what should we have for hot dishes?

W：Our special hot dishes are Sweet and Sour Pork, Boiled Fish and today's specialty is Fried and Spicy Shrimps. They really taste good.

M：OK，we'll also take them.

W：What would you like to drink? (Show the wine list to Mary and her friends.) We have Beijing Beer, Great Wall red wine and white wine. They are all well-known in China.

M：What's Wuliangye?

W：Wuliangye is one of the best liquors in China. It's strong but never goes to the head as most liquors do.

M：Really? We'd like to try a cup. And I need some tea. It's said that China is the homeland of tea.

W: Which tea would you prefer to have, Longjing Tea or Maojian Tea?

M: Longjing Tea, please.

W: Fine, Madam. Anything else?

M: No, thank you.

W: OK. Your dishes will be served as soon as possible.

Notes

1. a wide variety of… 各种各样的

2. Our special hot dishes are Sweet and Sour Pork, Boiled Fish and today's special-ty is Fried and Spicy Shrimps.　我们的热菜中比较有特色的是糖醋里脊、水煮鱼，今天的特价菜是香辣虾。

3. It's strong but never goes to the head as most liquors do.　（五粮液）酒味香醇且不易喝醉。

Dialogue Four

（Henry and his friend Joel go to a western food restaurant for supper. They plan to enjoy a fantastic meal together and ask the waiter to order the food.）

（W＝waiter　　H＝Henry　　J＝Joel）

W: Good evening, sir. What would you like to have? Would you like to order a full course meal or a la carte?

H: A la carte, please.

W: Are you ready to order, sir?

H: Yes. I want a beef steak with egg, a side salad and French onion soup.

W: Yes, sir. How would you like your steak?

H: Medium well.

W: Yes, medium well. And your egg, poached, fried or scrambled?

H: Poached, please.

W: Would you like some red wine, please?

H: No, thank you. I'll have some fruits. What fruit do you have today?

W: Today we have watermelons, pineapples, bananas, grapes and strawberries.

H: One plate of strawberries, please.

W：So French onion soup, a beef steak, medium well with a poached egg accompanied by a salad and one plate of strawberries. Thank you. How about you, sir? Our special for today is the mutton stewed with potato and a side serving of vegetables.

J：Sounds good. Just bring that dish for me.

W：OK. How would you like your vegetables done, boiled or stir-fried?

J：Stir-fried, please. For dessert, I'll take an ice cream.

W：What kind of ice cream would you like? We have strawberry, chocolate and vanilla.

J：Vanilla, please. We'd also like to have two Irish coffee afterwards.

W：OK. French onion soup, mutton stewed with potato and stir-fried vegetables, vanilla ice cream and two Irish coffee. It should take about ten minutes for the first course.

J：Thank you.

Notes

1. a full course meal or a la carte　一份套餐或点菜
   点菜有两种方式：一种是 a full course meal，意为"套餐、份饭，固定的几道菜肴"；另一种是 a la carte（法语），意为"按照菜单随意点菜"。

2. medium well　八成熟
   客人点牛排时，服务员要问清楚客人需要几成熟的。例如，rare（生的），medium（适中），well done（全熟）。

3. And your egg, poached, fried or scrambled?　请问您是要水煮荷包蛋、煎鸡蛋还是炒鸡蛋？

4. the mutton stewed with potato　羊肉炖土豆

5. boiled or stir-fried　水煮还是快炒

Part Ⅲ　Vocabulary & Useful Expressions

Ⅰ. Useful Words

cuisine　*n.* 烹饪，烹调风格

distinctive　*adj.* 有特色的，与众不同的

typical　*adj.* 典型的，象征性的

banquet *n.* 宴会

poultry *n.* 家禽，禽肉

seafood *n.* 海产品

dessert *n.* 餐后甜点

snack *n.* 小吃

toast *n.* 吐司面包，烤面包片

recommend *v.* 推荐，介绍

sauce *n.* 调味汁，酱汁

contrast *v.* 和……形成对比

tender *adj.* 柔软的，嫩的

crisp *adj.* 脆的

sour *adj.* 酸的

rip *v.* 撕，剥

stir *v.* 搅动

nip *v.* 夹，捏

delightful *adj.* 令人愉快的

dressing *n.* 调味品

scented *adj.* 芳香的

organic *adj.* 有机的

digestion *n.* 消化

herb *n.* 草药

Beijing Roast Duck 北京烤鸭

jasmine tea 茉莉花茶

medicinal food 药膳

candy sugar 冰糖

food tonic 食补

medicine tonic 药补

Ⅱ. Useful Expressions

1. Have you booked a table?

   您预订餐桌了吗?

2. Do you have a reservation?

   您预订过了吗?

3. Have you got a table for two, please?

请问有两个人的桌子吗？

4. Could you arrange me a table now?

能不能给我安排一张桌子？

5. Would you care to have a drink in the lounge while waiting?

您要不要边在休息室等边喝点什么？

6. Would you like to see the menu?

您需要看菜单吗？

7. I'd like to have...

我想要······

8. Is there anything else you would like to have?

您还需要什么别的吗？

9. Anything good for this evening?

今晚有什么好吃的吗？

10. Would you like something to drink?

您想喝什么？

11. Could you give us a brief description of the Chinese cuisine?

你能不能向我们大致介绍一下中国菜？

12. Well，we have no idea of the food here. Can you recommend some to us?

噢，我对这里的食物不太熟悉，你能为我们推荐几个吗？

13. What would you like to go with your steak?

您的牛排配什么菜呢？

14. Here are your appetizers.

这是您的开胃菜。

15. Are you used to the food here?

您吃得惯这里的饭菜吗？

16. This is not what I asked for，I'm afraid.

这道菜恐怕不是我要的。（上错菜）

17. Here is the bill. The total amount is...

这是您的账单，一共是······

18. Here is your change.

这是找给您的钱。

Part IV   Reading Materials

 **Passage One**

Chinese Cuisine

Chinese cuisine enjoys a high reputation in the world. "Fashion in Europe, living in America and eating in China. " This sentence is a testament to the popularity of Chinese cuisine around the world. Chinese cookery has evolved over centuries, forming a rich cultural content. It is characterized by fine selection of ingredients, precise processing, particular care for the amount of heat and substantial nourishment.

All chefs of the Chinese kitchens, professional or in the home, make great efforts to get harmony of seeing, smelling and tasting so that each dish has its unique features contrasted and balanced if it is a dinner of many dishes, be it 3, 6, 9 or 12. The flavors must not be too special, yet subtle enough to meet the tastes of those dinings. Dishes may be prepared quickly or much longer, but the final goal is to share with the guests the play on the cater's real and imagined visions of the dishes and its ingredients.

Due to China's diverse climate, products and customs, cooking and tastes vary from region to region. Generally speaking, Chinese cuisine can be roughly grouped according to the country's four major regions: the south, famous for the Cantonese cuisine (Guangdong cooking); the northern plains, with Shandong cuisine as its representative; the fertile east, typically known as Huaiyang cuisine and the west, renowned for Sichuan cuisine.

Including Jinan cuisine and Jiaodong cuisine, Shandong cuisine is generally pure-flavored, tasting somewhat salty, as well as fresh, tender, fragrant and crisp. The dishes feature choice of materials, adept slicing techniques and perfect cooking skills. Shallots and garlic are frequently used as seasonings, so Shandong dishes also taste pungent. The typical menu items for Shandong cuisine are Bird's Nest Soup, Yellow River Carp in Sweet and Sour Sauce.

Canton (Guangdong) is perhaps the most famous area for cooking. Long, warm and wet days throughout the year create the perfect environment for cultivating almost everything. The coast provides ample seafood. Since the local produce is so abundant and gorgeous, the cooking highlights its freshness, relying less on loud sauces and deep frying. All the vegetables, poultry and ingredients have to be fresh. Steaming and stir-frying are more commonly applied to preserve the natural flavor. The timing on the cooking is very important. Dishes must not be overcooked, and the texture of the food has to be just right with the freshness and tenderness still remaining. Soup is necessary in Cantonese cuisine, which includes different ingredients and herbs and is boiled to a rich and tasty soup before served. The typical menu items in Cantonese cuisine are Shark Fin Soup, Steamed Sea Bass and Roasted Piglet.

Huaiyang cuisine, also called Jiangsu cuisine, is popular in the lower reaches of the Yangtze River. Using fish and crustaceans as the main ingredients, it pays much more attention to their freshness. Its carving techniques are delicate and well-known. Cooking techniques are stewing, braising, roasting and simmering. The artistic shape and bright colors add more value to the dishes. Stewed Crab with Clear Soup, Squirrel with Mandarin Fish and Crystal Meat are the most famous menu items.

Sichuan cuisine is characterized by its numerous varieties of delicacies and strong flavors and is best known for being spicy-hot. It emphasizes the use of chili, red pepper and hot oil. Garlic, ginger and fermented soybean are also used in the cooking process. It is said that it consists of more than 5,000 dishes of which over 300 are very well-known to the people, so it is not exaggerated for the saying that one who doesn't experience Sichuan cuisine has never really reached China. The most famous menu items are Mapo Tofu, Boiled Fish, Ants Climbing a Tree, Kong Pau Chicken, and Twice Cooked Pork Slices.

The characteristic flavors of China's four major cuisines can be summed up in the following expression: "The light southern cuisine, the salty northern cuisine, the sweet eastern cuisine and the spicy western cuisine. " It is no exaggeration to say that Chinese cuisine is dainty in its items, esthetics, atmosphere and effects.

Notes

1. reputation *n.* 名誉，名声
2. testament *n.* 证明，证据
3. evolve *v.* 演变
4. ingredient *n.* 原料

5. substantial   *adj.* 大量的，丰富的

6. nourishment   *n.* 营养

7. harmony   *n.* 和谐

8. flavor   *n.* 风味，口味

9. diverse   *adj.* 多种多样的

10. vary   *v.* 改变，变化

11. region   *n.* 地区

12. fragrant   *adj.* 芳香的，有香味的

13. adept   *adj.* 精通的，巧妙的

14. shallot   *n.* 大葱

15. seasoning   *n.* 调味品

16. pungent   *adj.* 辛辣的

17. abundant   *adj.* 丰富的，充裕的

18. highlight   *v.* 对……加以特别的注意

19. texture   *n.* 质地，材料

20. crustacean   *n.* 贝类食物

21. characterize   *v.* 以……为特点

22. delicacy   *n.* 精美；美味佳肴

23. emphasize   *v.* 强调

24. ferment   *v.* 使发酵

25. dainty   *adj.* 精美的

26. esthetics   *n.* 美学

27. due to   由于

28. be renowned for   以……著名

29. apply...to...   把……应用于……

30. consist of   包括

31. rely on   依靠，依赖

32. sum up   归纳，总结

33. Bird's Nest Soup   燕窝羹

34. Yellow River Carp in Sweet and Sour Sauce   糖醋黄河鲤鱼

35. Shark Fin Soup   鱼翅羹

36. Steamed Sea Bass   清蒸石斑鱼

37. Roasted Piglet   烤乳猪

38. Stewed Crab with Clear Soup   清汤醉蟹

39. Squirrel with Mandarin Fish   松鼠鳜鱼

40. Crystal Meat　水晶肴肉

41. Mapo Tofu　麻婆豆腐

42. Boiled Fish　水煮鱼

43. Ants Climbing a Tree　蚂蚁上树

44. Kong Pau Chicken　宫保鸡丁

45. Twice Cooked Pork Slices　回锅肉

American Table Etiquettes

There is a famous saying, "The way to a man's heart is through his stomach." A girl should cook good meals if she wants to master her boyfriend's heart. Although this is a joke, to some degree, it has some reasonable factors because people cannot love without food and they put great importance to food whether in the west or in the east. However, different countries have different etiquettes. What is polite in China may not be welcomed in other countries. The following knowledge and rules will guide you enjoy American food when you are dining with your foreign friends.

Table Setting

● Bread or salad plates are to the left of the main plate, beverage glasses are to the right. If small bread knives are present, put them across the bread plate with the handle pointing to the right.

● Modern etiquette provides the smallest numbers and types of utensils necessary for dining. Even if some utensils are needed, hosts should not have more than three of them on either side of the plate before a meal. If extra utensils are needed, they may be brought to the table along with later courses.

● If a salad course is served early in the meal, the salad fork should be further from the main course fork, both set on the left. If a soup is served, the spoon is set on the right, further from the plate than the knife. Dessert utensils, a small fork and teaspoon should be placed above the main plate horizontally, or served with the dessert. For most restaurants, they may not follow these rules, instead setting a uniform complement of utensils at each seat.

● If a wine glass and a water glass are set, the wine glass is on the right directly above the knife. The water glass is to the left of the wine glass at a 45 degree angle, closer to the diner.

● Hosts should always provide cloth napkins to the guests. When paper napkins are provided, they should be treated the same as cloth napkin, thus should not be balled up or torn.

● Coffee or tea cups are placed to the right of the table setting, or above the setting to the right if space is limited. The cup's handle should be pointing right.

General Manners While Dining

● When a dish is offered from a serving dish (family style), as the traditional manner, the food may be passed around or served by a host or staff. If passed, you should pass on the serving dish to the next person in the same direction as the other dishes are being passed. Place the serving dish on your left, take some, and pass to the person next to you. You should consider how much is on the serving dish and not take more than a proportional amount so that everyone may have. If you do not care for any of the dish, pass it to the next person without comment. If being served by a single person, the server should ask if the guest would like any of the dish. The guest may say, "Yes, please" or "No, thank you".

● When serving, serve from the left and pick up the dish from the right. Beverages, however, are to be both served and as well as removed from the right-hand side.

● Eat soup noiselessly from the side of the spoon. When there is a small amount left, you may lift the front end of the dish slightly with your free hand to make more collection of soup with the spoon.

● If you are having difficulty getting food onto your fork, use a small piece of bread or your knife to help you. Never use your finger or thumb.

● It is acceptable not to accept all offerings and not to finish all the food onto your plate. No one should ask why another doesn't want any of a dish or why he hasn't finished a serving.

● Chew with your mouth closed. Do not slurp, talk with food in your mouth, or make loud or unusual noises while eating. Frequent clinking of utensils is not polite.

● Say "Excuse me" or "Excuse me, I'll be right back" before leaving the table. Do not say frankly that you are going to the restroom.

● If food must be removed from the mouth for some reason, it should be done by using the toothpick as well as the help of a napkin to cover the mouth if possible.

Using Utensils

● The fork in America should be used in the left hand while cutting, switch the right hand to pick up and eat a piece of food.

● Unless a knife stand is provided, the knife should be placed on the edge of your plate when not in use and should face inward.

● When courses are served, use your silverware from the outside moving inward towards the main plate. Dessert utensils are either above the main plate or served with dessert.

At the End of the Meal

● When you have finished your meal, place all used utensils onto your plate together on the right side pointing up, so the waiter knows you have finished.

● When your meal is finished, do not place the used napkin directly on your dinner plate. Leave it on the table next to the left of your plate when you leave during or at the end of a meal.

● Wait for your host to rise before getting up from a dinner party table.

● Once dessert or after-dinner coffee is served, be careful not to overstay. The person who wishes to end the party should rise and say, "This is a nice evening dinner. We hope we can see each other again soon."

Notes

1. The way to a man's heart is through his stomach.　抓住男人的胃也就抓住了男人的心。

2. When paper napkins are provided, they should be treated the same as cloth napkin, thus should not be balled up or torn.　如果提供的是纸餐巾（在没有布餐巾的情况下），同样不能撕碎或弄乱。

Part Ⅴ　Skill Training

Ⅰ. Matches.

a. cuisine   1. 充裕的，充足的

b. nourishment   2. 美味佳肴

c. abundant

d. diverse

e. characterize

f. delicacy

g. etiquette

h. utensil

i. frequent

j. switch

3. 器具，器物

4. 烹饪

5. 频繁的

6. 营养

7. 繁多的，各式各样的

8. 变换，转换

9. 以……为特点

10. 礼仪，礼节

Ⅱ. **Choices.**

harmony	highlight	evolve	apply...to	consist of	reputation
vary	proportional	uniform	be renowned for		

1. The American constitution was planned while the British constitution was _____.

2. Payment should be _____ to the amount of work done by workers.

3. This book store has an excellent _____ for fair dealing.

4. The French _____ their wonderful cooking.

5. The rows of these houses were _____ in appearance.

6. The designer's aim is to produce a(n) _____ of shape and texture.

7. The results of this research can be _____ new technology developments.

8. This TV programme _____ the problems caused by unemployment.

9. The company _____ ten members to run it.

10. Teachers should learn to _____ their lessons to make them more interesting.

Ⅲ. **Translate the following sentences into Chinese.**

1. Different countries have different notions about table manners— how people behave while they are eating.

2. Now, people can still feel the importance of tea from the Chinese saying, "Firewood, rice, oil, salt, soy sauce, vinegar and tea are the seven necessities to begin a day."

3. When you eat, you should not lean towards the plate, but bring the knife, fork or spoon towards you.

4. Chopsticks are used either to grasp the food or to push it from plate to mouth.

They are available for all purposes except eating soup or ice cream.

5. There are many Chinese snacks that foreign guests enjoy, such as dumplings (jiaozi), spring rolls, rice balls, zongzi and moon cakes.

Ⅳ. Translate the Chinese in brackets into English.

1. Chinese cuisine is characterized by fine selection of ingredients, precise processing, particular care for the amount of heat and _____ (营养丰富).

2. _____ (由于中国气候复杂多变), products and customs, cooking and tastes vary from region to region.

3. _____ (口味特点) of China's four major cuisines can be summed up in the following expression.

4. For most restaurants, they may not _____ (遵循这些规则), instead setting a uniform complement of utensils at each seat.

5. Unless a knife stand is provided, the knife should _____ (放在盘子边) when not in use and should face inward.

Ⅴ. Situational play.

Situation 1

Suppose you are a tour guide for a group of American tourists to travel Hangzhou. At noon, you lead them to a famous local restaurant for dinner. Please try to say as much as possible for the following items:

(1) Introduce some special dishes about Hangzhou;

(2) Introduce some drinks about Hangzhou;

(3) Understand different guests' likes and dislikes for food and drinks;

(4) Order the meal;

(5) Recommend chopsticks and explain how to use them.

Situation 2

As a tour guide, you lead a group of Chinese people to travel America. Now you are planning to take them to a formal banquet, so you try to tell them some American etiquettes while dining and help them do some practice.

(1) Introduce how to use knife and fork;

(2) Introduce some important American etiquettes for dinning;

(3) Ask guests to do some practice: being seated → eating → drinking → asking for short leave → finishing meal.

Part Ⅵ　Knowledge Expansion

境外如何支付小费

　　小费是指在一些国家顾客对从事服务性工作的人员给予一定的合理酬劳，是一种酬谢方式。小费在许多国家是服务人员的一项重要收入。譬如在泰国，普通工薪阶层的收入平均每月五六千泰铢，而饭店打扫房间的服务员每月的工资却只有 1 000 泰铢左右。因而住店客人给的小费，就成为他们维持正常生活的重要收入。客人付小费可以表达的涵义颇为丰富。它既能代表客人对服务人员付出的劳动的尊重，也可以表达客人对服务工作的一种肯定和感激之情。从另一个层面来说，付小费被视为一种社交礼仪，体现了客人的文化修养和文明礼貌。

小费要付给谁？

　　一般而言，除了对酒店打扫房间的服务员一定要给小费外，对许多给客人提供特殊服务的人也要付小费，这里的特殊服务是指不属于客房服务范畴的服务。例如饭店的行李员如果笑盈盈地帮你将行李提到了房间，那就绝不仅仅意味着热情，你理所应当付小费给他。同样，出租车司机把你送到目的地，你在计价器显示金额的基础上要增加一点当做小费。

怎样付小费？

　　付小费亦有一些技巧和惯例。给打扫房间的服务员的小费，在离开房间时放在显眼的位置即可。小费忌放在枕头底下，那样的话会被服务员认为是客人自己的东西忘了拿。如果能在小费的旁边留一张"THANK YOU"字条，会备受服务员的欢迎和尊重。如果要当面付小费给行李员，那最好是与他握手表示感谢的同时将小费暗暗给他。给导游、司机的小费，则要由团员一起交齐后放到信封里，由一位代表当众给他们。当面付小费时最忌给硬币。

付多少小费合适？

　　到不同的国家去旅行，除天气、景观、风俗等要事先了解之外，小费也是必须事先弄明白的一件事情。既然是小费，其数目自然不必太大。一般情况下，客人支付明码标价的 10%～15% 作为小费是比较适宜的。比如在泰国享受完泰式按摩，收银员开票收取 400 泰铢，那么你再付 40～50 泰铢给按摩服务生就可以。

注意事项

　　1. 就餐是产生小费最多的场合。一般来说，快餐和自助餐不给小费，而特色菜肴和专项服务要给小费。

● 在飞机上就餐不给小费，但是如果你愿意给，没人会拒绝。

● 在酒店里吃自助早餐不给小费，但是在北美唐人街喝早茶，一般要付小费。

● 街头流动售货车的食品无须付小费。

● 游乐场里的饮食区一般不给小费。

● 厨师不停展示厨艺，服务人员不停送免费的面包、咖啡、饮料，之后侍者还不停问你需要什么，注意一定要付小费，否则旁边的人会觉得你很没礼貌。

● 中餐馆里的"点菜"，吃过后要付小费。小费是侍者的重要收入来源，有的侍者甚至在签约时不要老板的基本工资，他的收入百分之百靠小费。

2. 酒店、机场以及一些特殊场合也是需要付小费的。

● 大酒店的房间清理，一般要付小费。行李员帮你提行李到房间，一定要付小费。

● 驾车到酒店时要停车，如果是酒店的侍者帮你停车，要付小费。

● 机场的行李员帮你推行李，一般要付小费。

● 特殊游览如马车游一定要付小费，即便讲好价钱后，也要再多付一点当做小费。

● 个人的街艺表演，如果观看就要付小费，不观看可以匆匆而过。

Chapter 5

Transportation

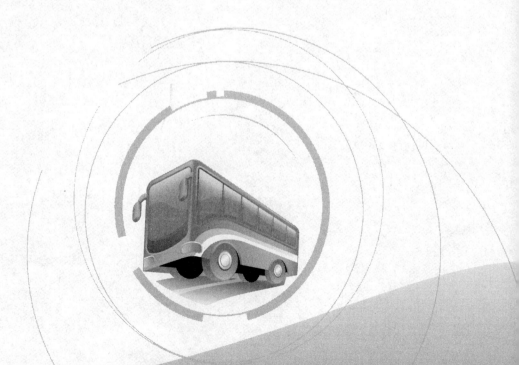

Part I   Lead-in

【本章简介】

本章介绍旅游中的交通环节，针对乘火车、乘飞机等交通方式，设计了多个真实的场景。由于在实际应用中，飞机旅行对英语口语的要求更高，应用更广泛，因此本章的重点为乘飞机英语，通过原汁原味的客舱英语、真实的机场情景、实用丰富的民航知识来提高和锻炼学生的口语交际能力。

【教学目标】

1. 掌握与交通工具、机场、客舱服务相关的专业词汇及用语；
2. 熟悉相应的服务流程，并能熟练地用英语表达；
3. 了解民航知识。

【背景知识】

随着中国旅游市场的蓬勃发展，越来越多的旅行机构开辟了国际旅游线路，越来越多的中国游客走出国门，同时大量的外国游客也进入中国境内观光。在此背景下，要提高旅游中交通环节的服务质量，就要求我们提高在此方面的英语交际能力。

Part II   Situational Dialogues

Dialogue One

Asking for Information

(P＝Peter   A＝agent)

P：I'd like to take a trip to Salt Lake City. Can you tell me how I could get there?

A: Sure. The fastest way is to fly. It takes about one hour, and there are 5 flights a day.

P: That sounds very quick.

A: Of course. But you have to go from Denver to the airport to take the plane, and when you get off the plane, you have to go from the airport to the city. That will add about 3 hours to your trip.

P: Oh, I hadn't thought of that. How much does it cost?

A: Let me check. It is about 280 dollars for a round trip.

P: 280 dollars? Sounds a little expensive. What about the train? How long does it take?

A: It takes 7 hours and about 100 dollars for a round trip.

P: That's much cheaper.

A: Definitely. It's as comfortable as airplane. And it arrives at the center of the city.

P: Great. What about other ways to get there?

A: You can rent a car. I could give you a very good deal, about 40 dollars a day with unlimited mileage.

P: Unlimited mileage? Well, how long will it take to drive from Denver to the Salt Lake City?

A: About eight hours by express way.

P: It would be fun to enjoy the scenery along the way. Thank you for your help. I'll call you in a day or two.

Dialogue Two

Booking an Air Ticket

(C=booking office clerk   P=passenger)

C: China Southern Airline. Can I help you?

P: Are there any flight to New York on Sunday?

C: If you excuse me for a second, I'll check. Yes, there are flights. How do you wish to fly, sir? Economy or first class? Window seat or aisle seat?

P: Economy and window seat, please.

C: Do you want food?

P: I'd like to have vegetarian food, please.

C: Sure, sir. Which day do you prefer?

P: The day after tomorrow.

C: Would you like a morning or afternoon flight?

P: I want to take the ten o'clock flight, please.

C: How many tickets do you want?

P: I'd like to book two tickets, please.

C: What's your last name?

P: It's Baltimore. My first name is Fred.

C: OK, sir. Two tickets to New York at 10 a. m. on May 9th. Is it right?

P: Yes, it is. How much is it?

C: It's altogether 6,200 dollars with fuel surcharge and airport construction fee.

P: Can I pay by credit card?

C: Yes, please. ...Well, your flight is OK now.

Notes

1. economy class   经济舱

2. first class   头等舱

3. window seat or aisle seat   靠窗的座位还是靠过道的座位

4. vegetarian   *adj.* 素食的，只有蔬菜的   *n.* 素食的人，素食主义者

5. surcharge   *n.* 附加费；额外费用

 **Dialogue Three**

Boarding Pass

(S=airport staff   P=passenger)

S: Good morning.

P: Good morning. Can I check in here for CA2963 to New York?

S: Yes, may I have your ticket and passport, please?

P: Here you are.

S：Do you have any baggage to check?

P：Yes，I have 2 pieces of baggage.

S：Please put your baggage on the convey or belt one by one.

P：OK. Could I take this briefcase as my hand baggage?

S：That's all right. What kind of seat do you prefer?

P：I'd like to have a window seat.

S：I'm sorry. No window seats are available. Will the aisle seat be all right?

P：That's okay.

S：Here are your ticket and passport，and here are your boarding pass and baggage checks.

P：Thank you very much.

S：Have a nice trip.

Notes

1. check in　办理登机手续；（旅客登机前）验票并办理登机牌

2. Do you have any baggage to check?　您有行李要托运吗?

3. briefcase　*n.* 行李箱

4. boarding pass　登机牌

Dialogue Four

Check-in

(S＝airport staff　　P＝passenger)

S：Good afternoon. Can I help you?

P：Yes, I'd like to check in.

S：May I see your ticket and passport，please?

P：Here you are.

S：How many pieces of baggage do you have to check?

P：Just one. I'll take the suitcase and backpack on board myself.

S：You have to check that suitcase too，sir.

P：Why? I have something fragile in it.

S：It's too big to be a carry-on.

P: Really? In that case, let me first take out what is fragile.

S: That's fine.

P: What about the backpack? Can I carry it with me?

S: I'm sorry, sir. You have to check your backpack, too. There is a bottle of beef sauce in it, right?

P: Yes, there is. What's wrong with it?

S: There is too much oil in the sauce, so you can't take it to the plane.

P: What if I put the beef sauce in my suitcase? Then I could bring my backpack with me.

S: Of course, sir. That's a good idea.

P: OK, done.

S: Here are your passport, boarding pass and luggage checks. Have a nice trip.

 **Dialogue Five**

Security Check

(S=airport staff   P=passenger)

S: Excuse me, sir. Please walk through the metal detector.

P: Oh, sorry.

S: Please put all metal objects into the plastic bag.

P: I have a bunch of keys and some coins. Is that OK?

S: I'm sorry. You need to take all your metal objects out.

P: Here you are.

S: Alright, sir. Here are your objects and belongings. Be sure to take all of them with you.

 **Dialogue Six**

On the Plane

(P=passenger   A=flight attendant)

79

P: Can you show me where my seat is?

A: Your seat is over there, 20C, the twentieth row, aisle seat.

(After a while.)

A: Your dinner, sir.

P: Thank you.

A: Would you care for some wine to go with your meal?

P: That'll be great.

A: Your wine, sir.

P: Thank you very much. Can I have coffee later?

A: Yes, I'll bring it after dinner. Is there anything else I can do for you?

P: Can I have a blanket, please? I feel a little cold.

A: I'm sorry. There isn't any at this moment. Can you wait for a little while?

P: Sure.

Notes

1. flight attendant   空乘人员
2. Would you care for some wine to go with your meal?   您想来点酒配您的饭菜吗?

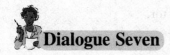

Dialogue Seven

Customs Examination

(O=customs officer   H=Henry)

O: May I see your passport, please?

H: Sure, here you are. And this is the declaration form.

O: What is the purpose of your visit?

H: I'm here on business.

O: This visa is good for two weeks. How long will you be staying?

H: For ten days.

O: And you will do some traveling while you are here?

H: Yes, I want to spend a couple of days traveling. I have friends there I will visit.

O: What do you have in the bag?

H: Just a camera, clothes, and some books.

O: Would you mind opening the bag for me?

H: Alright.

O: OK. Enjoy your trip, sir.

H: Thank you very much.

Notes

1. customs   *n.* 海关
2. declaration form   过关申请表
3. on business   公干，出差
4. visa   *n.* 签证

Part Ⅲ   Vocabulary & Useful Expressions

Ⅰ. Useful Words

baggage/luggage   *n.* 行李

lavatory   *n.* 盥洗室

occupied   *adj.* 在使用的，无空闲的，已占用的

vacant   *adj.* 无人，空的

stewardess   *n.* 女空服员

steward   *n.* 男空服员

concourse   *n.* 中央大厅

flight/flying   *n.* 飞行

ramp   *n.* 扶梯

altitude/height   *n.* 高度

circling   *n.* 盘旋

speed/velocity   *n.* 速度

ceiling　*n.* 上升限度

airsick　*n.* 晕机

landing　*n.* 着陆

climbing　*n.* 爬升

international airport　国际机场

domestic airport　国内机场

international flight　国际班机

domestic flight　国内班机

airport terminal　机场候机楼

international departure　国际航班出港

domestic departure　国内航班出站

international terminal　国际航班候机楼

domestic terminal　国内航班候机楼

scheduled time　预计时间

actual time　实际时间

departure time　起飞时间

passport control immigration　护照检查处

transfer correspondence　中转处

money/currency exchange　货币兑换处

currency exchange shop　货币兑换店

exchange rate　汇率

traveler's check　旅行支票

first class　头等舱

business class　商务舱

economy class　经济舱

flight number　航班号

one-way ticket　单程机票

round-trip ticket　来回机票

air hostess　女空服员

customs service area　海关申报处

currency declaration　货币申报

duty-free shop　免税店

duty-free items　免税商品

dutiable goods　需课税商品

checked baggage　托运的行李

baggage claim area　行李领取处

carry-on baggage　随身行李

baggage tag　行李牌

luggage claim　行李领取处

luggage cart　行李推车

plane ticket　飞机票

airline operation　航空业务

alternate airfield　备用机场

landing field　停机坪

control tower　控制台

jet way　登机道

air-bridge　旅客桥

visitor terrace　迎送平台

loading bridge　候机室至飞机的连接通路，桥式起重机

airline coach service　航空公司汽车服务

shuttle bus　机场内来往班车

bumpy flight　不平稳的飞行

smooth flight　平稳的飞行

extra flight　加班

non-stop flight　连续飞行

forced landing　迫降

cruising speed　巡航速度

top speed　最高速度

night service　夜航

to taxi along　滑行

to face the wind　迎风

air route/air line　航线

connecting flight　衔接航班

direct flight/straight flight　直飞

to rock/to toss/to bump　颠簸

to lose height/to fly low　降低

to take off/take-off 起飞

to board a plane/to get into a plane 上飞机

to get off a plane/to alight from a plane 下飞机

Ⅱ. Useful Expressions

i. By Train

1. You can get a train from Beijing Station.

   你可以从北京站坐车。

2. Which platform does the train leave?

   火车从哪个站台发车？

3. Trains leave from Platform 8.

   火车从 8 号站台发车。

4. How many trains are there from Shanghai to Hangzhou?

   从上海到杭州有几班车？

5. There are 2 trains per day.

   每天有两班车。

6. When/What time do trains leave?

   什么时候发车？

7. The train leaves at 8：45 p. m. from Zhengzhou and arrives in Beijing at 6：10 a. m. the next morning.

   火车晚上 8：45 从郑州出发，第二天上午 6：10 到达北京。

8. What sorts of trains are there?

   有什么车？

9. There is a fast/slow train to the town.

   到城里有快车/慢车。

10. How much is the ticket?

    车票多少钱？

11. A first class single costs 200 yuan.

    头等的单程票是 200 元。

12. A second class return costs 160 yuan.

    二等的往返票是 160 元。

13. How long does the journey take?

    整个行程多长时间？

14. The journey takes about 5 hours.

    本次行程大约需要 5 个小时。

15. Where do I have to change?

    我在哪儿换车?

16. To get to Shenzhen，you must change at Changsha.

    要到深圳，您必须在长沙转车。

ii. By Air

1. Are the flights to Huston non-stop?

    飞机直达休斯敦吗?

2. Are there any planes to Shanghai next Monday?

    下周一有到上海的飞机吗?

3. Can I break my journey at Tokyo?

    我可以中途在东京停留吗?

4. Can I fly to Paris on Sunday?

    星期日有飞往巴黎的飞机吗?

5. Could you tell me about flights to Washington D. C. ?

    能告诉我飞往华盛顿特区的班机情况吗?

6. Do you have any flights to Denver this afternoon?

    下午有飞往丹佛的航班吗?

7. Do I have to change planes in Hong Kong?

    我必须在香港转机吗?

8. How many flights are there to Florida?

    去佛罗里达有几趟航班?

9. How much is the round trip?

    往返机票多少钱?

10. How much luggage can I take with me?

    我可以随身携带多少行李?

11. How many pieces of baggage do you have to check?

    您要托运几件行李?

12. Just one. I'll take the suitcase on board myself.

    就一件，这个手提箱我随身带上飞机。

13. How much should I pay for the overweight?

    我应该付多少超重费?

14. What time am I supposed to check-in?

我应该什么时候办理登机手续？

15. When can I board the plane?

我什么时候可以登机？

16. I want a first class open return, please.

我要一张不定期的头等返程票。

17. Book me two economy class seats to Sanya, please.

请给我订两张去三亚的经济舱机票。

18. How do you want to fly, coach or first class?

您想买什么票，二等还是头等？

19. I'm sorry. We are all booked up for Flight CZ3340.

对不起，CZ3340 航班已全部预订完了。

20. Here is your tickets and boarding card.

这是您的机票和登机牌。

21. Do I go through the red/green channel?

我需要走红色/绿色通道吗？

22. Your luggage can weigh up to 30 kilos.

您最多可以携带 30 千克的行李。

23. Do you have luggage to check in?

您有要托运的行李吗？

24. You have to check this item of luggage.

您这件行李必须托运。

25. Can you tell me what time we're arriving in London?

请问几点到达伦敦？

26. I'd like to check three pieces of luggage and I also have carry-on luggage.

我想托运三件行李，我也有需要随身携带的行李。

27. Please walk through the metal detector.

请走过金属探测器。

28. Can you help me to get to Gate 20, please?

请问 20 号登机口在哪里？

29. Good morning, Madam. Welcome aboard.

早上好，女士。欢迎登机。

30. May I introduce myself? I'm Alfred Benson, the chief purser of this flight.

请允许我作自我介绍。我是艾尔弗雷德·本森，本次航班的乘务长。

31. Good morning, sir. Welcome aboard. Business class or economy?

早上好，先生，欢迎登机。您是商务舱还是经济舱？

32. Follow me, please. Your seat is in the middle of the cabin.

请跟我来，您的座位在客舱中部。

33. An aisle seat on the left side—here you are, sir.

是左边靠走廊座位——这是您的座位，先生。

34. I'm afraid you are in the wrong seat. 20C is just two rows behind on the other side of the aisle.

恐怕您坐错位子了，20C 要往后坐两排，在走廊的另一侧。

35. The plane is about to take off. Please don't walk around in the cabin.

飞机马上要起飞了，请不要在客舱内走动。

36. An oxygen mask will come down from overhead in case of emergency.

一遇到紧急情况，头顶上的氧气罩就会放下来。

37. The plane is taking off. Please fasten your seat belt.

飞机正在起飞，请系好安全带。

38. The plane is slowing down/gaining speed.

飞机正在减速/加速。

39. We'll land in about ten minutes.

十分钟后我们就要着陆了。

40. Let me push the call button and get the flight attendant to help you.

让我按一下呼叫按钮，让空乘人员来帮助你。

iii. At the Customs

1. May I see your passport, please?

请出示您的护照。

2. Do you have your visa?

您有签证吗？

3. What's your citizenship?

请问您的国籍是什么？

4. Have you got your entry documents?

您有没有带入境证件？

5. Passport and declaration, please.

请出示护照和报关单。

6. Where is your vaccination certificate?

您的预防接种证明书在哪儿?

7. Anything to declare?

有需要报关的物品吗?

8. Please open your briefcase.

请把您的包打开。

9. This is your dutiable article.

这个物品要缴税。

10. I don't know what things are dutiable. Do I have to pay duty on the things for my own use?

我不知道什么物品需要缴税。我的个人用品需要缴税吗?

11. No, you don't have to pay duty on your personal belongings.

不,您不需要为私人用品缴税。

12. Anything dutiable?

有需要缴税的物品吗?

13. Do you have anything dutiable, sir?

先生,有需要缴税的物品吗?

14. You are entitled to a duty-free exemption of 100 dollars article free. So you don't have to pay any duty this time.

您可以有 100 美元的免税额度,所以这次您不用缴税。

Part Ⅳ   Reading Materials

How to Check in at the Airport?

Here are four steps for you to follow when you are going to take a plane.

Step 1: Maintain a secure place for all your travel documents. Have your travel itinerary, tickets, passport, identification and visa all in one place. Make sure that you have any customs forms filled out in advance and stored. Also store any contact numbers of clients or friends that you will be meeting stored in this location. Make sure that this location is on your person or in your immediate control so that it can't be lost or stolen.

Step 2: Ensure you check with airport security before arriving at the airport for the list of items that you can't have in carry-on luggage. Many of the holdups at the airport security checks are for items clearly posted as not allowed on the airplane. Leave any tools or cosmetics that are flammable in your checked luggage or plan on replacing it when you arrive at your destination.

Step 3: Wear sensible clothes that you can quickly remove if necessary like slip-on shoes. Eliminate belts and apparel that has a lot of metal on it. These will trigger the scanners that you must pass through at the security check point.

Step 4: Make sure you allow enough time to arrive at your gate with your boarding pass (at least 15 minutes before your scheduled departure time). If you are required to check your luggage, add additional time. Best estimates are that you should be at your boarding gate no less than 30 minutes before departure time for domestic travel and one hour before any international travel destinations.

✑✑✑ Notes ✑✑✑

1. itinerary   *n.* 行程
2. identification   *n.* 身份证明
3. in advance   提前
4. client   *n.* 客户
5. holdup   *n. &v.* 停顿；交通管制
6. cosmetic   *n.* 化妆品，美容品
7. flammable   *adj.* 易燃的，可燃的
8. destination   *n.* 目的地
9. sensible   *adj.* 明智的；（服装等）朴素而实用的
10. slip-on shoes   便鞋
11. eliminate   *v.* 除掉；淘汰；摒弃
12. apparel   *n.* 服装
13. trigger   *n.* 扳机；引爆器；启动线路

Passage Two

Shanghai Expo and Guangzhou Asia Games Stimulate Tourism in China

The Shanghai Expo and the Guangzhou Asia Games, two of the most eye-catching events in China in 2010, both achieved record entries thanks to publicity and media exposure, and the encouragement of the government. Due to the large tourism flows, hotels, air transportation and travel retail all enjoyed healthy growth in 2010.

The New Five-year Strategic Tourism Plan Is Issued

A new strategic tourism plan was established by the China State Council at the end of 2009, which aims to speed up the development of tourism, and further promote the service industry to achieve leapfrog development. It also stresses that the greatest importance should be attached to domestic tourism, and efforts should be made to expedite its development.

Low-carbon Tourism

Low-carbon tourism has been brought into the spotlight for the first time by the China State Council. As required, local tourism offices will incorporate low-carbon tourism within their tourism development schemes in order to achieve a reduction in greenhouse gas emissions within the next five years. Issues such as the use of clean energy sources also have been put on the agenda.

Chinese Tourists Are Thought to Be a "Hot Commodity"

With strong GDP growth and rising disposable incomes in China, Chinese tourists have been identified as a "hot commodity" by more and more international tourism boards. As a result, total outbound tourist expenditure is expected to continue its strong growth over the forecast period.

Online Travel Retail Begins to Grow

Internet transactions in tourism in China are starting to increase, and Chinese consumers, especially the younger generation, are now becoming more comfortable purchasing online. In the past, Chinese consumers were generally reluctant to make online purchases, and mainly used the Internet to obtain travel information, because of the insecurity of online payment and concerns about buying on credit.

Notes

1. entry　　*n.*　入场；参加，出赛；进入权

2. exposure　　*n.*　暴露；揭露；曝光

3. strategic　　*adj.*　关键的；战略上的

4. China State Council　　中国国务院

5. leapfrog　　*n.*　跳背游戏；竞相提高　*v.*　交替前进；越过

6. be attached to　　附属于；与……有联系；喜爱

7. expedite　　*v.*　加快进展；迅速完成

8. low-carbon　　低碳
低碳是指较低（更低）的温室气体（以二氧化碳为主）排放。低碳的内涵为低碳社会、低碳经济、低碳生产、低碳消费、低碳生活、低碳城市、低碳社区、低碳家庭、低碳旅游、低碳文化、低碳哲学、低碳艺术、低碳音乐、低碳人生、低碳生存主义、低碳生活方式。其中，低碳经济和低碳生活是其核心内容。低碳经济，是以低能耗、低污染、低排放为基础的经济模式。低碳生活，就是把生活作息时间所耗用的能量尽量减少，从而减少二氧化碳的排放量。

9. spotlight　　*n.*　聚光灯；公众注意的中心

10. incorporate　　*v.*　包含，吸收；组成公司

11. scheme　　*n.*　计划，方案；计谋

12. greenhouse　　*n.*　温室；花房

13. emission　　*n.*　排放，散发

14. clean energy source　　清洁能源
清洁能源是不排放污染物的能源，它包括核能和可再生能源。可再生能源是指原材料可以再生的能源，如水能、风能、太阳能、生物能（沼气）、潮汐能等。可再生能源不存在能源耗竭的可能，因此日益受到许多国家的重视，尤其是能源短缺的国家。

15. agenda　　*n.*　议事日程，议程表

16. commodity　　*n.*　商品；有价值的物品

17. disposable income　　可支配收入；税后所得

18. board　　*n.*　木板；委员会，董事会

19. outbound　　*adj.*　开往外国的，向外的，出港的

20. expenditure　　*n.*　花费；支出额；消耗

21. transaction　　*n.*　处理，办理；交易

22. reluctant　　*adj.*　不情愿的；勉强的

23. on credit　　赊欠；赊购；赊销

Part Ⅴ Skill Training

Ⅰ. Matches.

a. business class　　　　　　　　1. 来回机票

b. economy class　　　　　　　　2. 海关

c. shuttle bus　　　　　　　　　 3. 经济舱

d. ticket confirm　　　　　　　　4. 机票确认

e. checked baggage　　　　　　　5. 商务舱

f. baggage claim area　　　　　　6. 行李领取处

g. carry-on baggage　　　　　　　7. 免税商品

h. round-trip ticket　　　　　　　8. 随身行李

i. duty-free items　　　　　　　　9. 托运的行李

j. customs　　　　　　　　　　　10. 摆渡车

Ⅱ. Translate the following sentences into Chinese.

1. Your passport and declaration card，please.

2. This is a souvenir that I'm taking to Taiwan.

3. Do you have anything to declare?

4. Book me two economy class seats to Sanya，please.

5. I'm sorry. We are all booked up for Flight CZ3340.

Ⅲ. Translate the following sentences into English.

1. 您必须为这件物品缴付税金。

2. 好了！请将这张申报表交给出口处的官员。

3. 早上好，女士。欢迎登机。

4. 您想买什么票，二等还是头等？

5. 您最多可以携带 30 千克的行李。

Ⅳ. Situational play.

Situation 1

You are an air ticket booking office staff. A guest comes to you and wants to book two tickets to Hong Kong on March 5th, but the tickets are booked up on that day.

Make a dialogue with your partner.

Situation 2

You are an airport staff. You are checking in for a passenger.

Part VI Knowledge Expansion

机场广播通知

1. 办理乘机手续通知

Ladies and Gentlemen, may I have your attention please? We are now ready for check-in for (supplementary) Flight CA2986 to Shanghai at counter No.17. Thank you!

前往上海的旅客请注意：您乘坐的（补班）CA2986 次航班现在开始办理乘机手续，请您到 17 号柜台办理。谢谢！

2. 推迟办理乘机手续通知

Ladies and Gentlemen, may I have your attention please? Due to

(1) the poor weather condition at our airport/

(2) the poor weather condition over the air route/

(3) the poor weather condition over Shanghai Airport/

(4) aircraft reallocation/

(5) the maintenance of the aircraft/

(6) the aircraft maintenance at our airport/

(7) the aircraft maintenance at Shanghai Airport/

(8) air traffic congestion/

(9) the close-down of Shanghai airport/

(10) communication trouble,

the (supplementary) Flight CA2986 to Shanghai has been delayed. The check-in for this flight will be postponed to 16:20. Please wait in the departure hall for further information. Thank you!

乘坐（补班）CA2986 次航班前往上海的旅客请注意：由于（1）本站天气达不到飞行标准/（2）航路天气达不到飞行标准/（3）上海天气达不到飞行标准/（4）飞机调配原因/（5）飞机机械原因/（6）飞机在本站出现机械故障/（7）飞机

在上海机场出现机械故障／（8）航行管制原因／（9）上海机场关闭／（10）通信原因，您乘坐的（补班）CA2986 次航班不能按时办理乘机手续，预计推迟到 16 点 20 分办理。请您在出发厅休息，等候通知。谢谢！

3. 催促办理乘机手续通知

Ladies and Gentlemen，may I have your attention please? Check-in for Flight CA3387 to Shanghai will be closed at 17：10. Passengers，who have not been checked in for this flight，please go to counter No. 29 immediately. Thank you!

前往上海的旅客请注意：您乘坐的 CA3387 次航班将在 17 点 10 分停止办理乘机手续。没有办理本次航班乘机手续的旅客，请马上到 29 号柜台办理。谢谢！

4. 正常登机通知

Ladies and Gentlemen，may I have your attention please? Flight MU7766 alternated from Shanghai to Sanya is now boarding. Would you please have your belongings and boarding passes ready and board the aircraft No. 17 through gate No. 4? We wish you a pleasant journey. Thank you!

由上海备降本站前往三亚的旅客请注意：您乘坐的 MU7766 次航班现在开始登机。请带好您的随身物品，出示登机牌，由 4 号登机口上 17 号飞机。祝您旅途愉快。谢谢！

5. 催促登机通知

Ladies and Gentlemen，may I have your attention please? Flight MU7766 to Sanya will take off soon. Please be quick to board through gate No. 4. This is the final call for boarding on Flight MU7766. Thank you!

前往三亚的旅客请注意：您乘坐的 MU7766 次航班很快就要起飞了，还没有登机的旅客请马上由 4 号登机口登机。这是 MU7766 次航班最后一次登机广播。谢谢！

6. 航班延误通知

Ladies and gentlemen，may I have your attention please? We regret to announce that Flight MU7765 to Shanghai cannot leave on schedule due to the aircraft maintenance at our airport. Would you please remain in the waiting hall and wait for further information? If you have any problems or questions，please contact with the service counter. Thank you!

前往上海的旅客请注意：我们抱歉地通知，您乘坐的 MU7765 次航班由于飞机在本站出现机械故障不能按时起飞。在此我们深表歉意，请您在候机厅休息，等候通知。如果您有什么要求，请与服务台联系。谢谢！

7. 正常航班预告

Ladies and Gentlemen，may I have your attention please? Flight CZ5327 from

Guangzhou will arrive here at 11:42. Thank you!

迎接旅客的各位请注意：由广州飞来本站的 CZ5327 次航班将于 11 点 42 分到达。谢谢！

8. 航班延误预告

Ladies and Gentlemen，may I have your attention please? We regret to announce that Flight CZ5327 from Guangzhou cannot arrive on schedule due to aircraft realloca- tion. This flight will be delayed to 13:30. Thank you!

迎接旅客的各位请注意：我们抱歉地通知，由广州飞来本站的 CZ5327 次航班由于飞机调配原因不能按时到达，预计到达本站的时间为 13 点 30 分。谢谢！

Chapter 6

Shopping

Part I Lead-in

【本章简介】

本章主要介绍旅游过程中很重要的一个环节——购物。读者通过情景对话以及延伸阅读等了解导游在游客购物过程中所起的作用，最后通过练习进一步了解并掌握导游业务方面的知识。

【教学目标】

1. 掌握与购物相关的专业词汇及用语；
2. 熟悉相应的购物流程，并能用英语熟练地表达；
3. 了解并熟悉中国传统的文化艺术；
4. 能够以恰当的方式引导客人购物。

【背景知识】

购物在整个旅游过程中占据重要的地位，游客购物心情的好坏会直接影响到整个旅程的成败。导游应当尽职尽责地为客人做好引导购物服务，耐心地提供尽可能多的帮助，帮助完成游客购物的心愿。购物应以游客自愿为原则，决不能强迫客人购物，更不能欺诈游客。

Part II Situational Dialogues

Dialogue One

(At the Souvenir Shop.)

(A＝shop assistant   T＝tourist)

A：Good morning, sir. Can I help you?

T：Yes, thank you. I'm especially interested in traditional Chinese paintings. Do

you have any good paintings?

A: Yes, we do. Do you prefer landscape or figure paintings?

T: That one with a beautiful lady seems good.

A: You've made a good choice. The lady's name is Diaochan. She was one of the most famous of the four beauties in ancient China.

T: It's really very nice. How much is it?

A: 260 yuan.

T: I'll take it. By the way, one of my friends likes porcelain wares very much. Could you recommend some to me?

A: (Pointing to a set of blue and white porcelain tea set.) This china tea set is unusual, it is made in Jingdezhen—the capital of porcelain.

T: It is extremely beautiful. I'm sure he will like it. How much do I owe you?

A: Two hundred and sixty yuan for the painting, three hundred and fifty yuan for the tea set. That's 610 yuan in all. Can I get you anything else?

T: That's all, thank you. Here is 700 yuan.

A: Here's the change. Thank you, sir. Have a nice trip.

Notes

1. landscape painting　风景画
2. figure painting　人物画
3. porcelain wares　瓷器

Dialogue Two

(Andy and Kelly go into an arts and crafts shop. They come to a counter.)

(S=sales girl　A=Andy　K=Kelly)

S: Can I be of any service to you?

A: I've been told that Chinese arts and crafts are famous for their excellent workmanship. We would like to take some home. What would you recommend?

S: There are over a thousand kinds of articles in our shop. For example, there is tri-colored pottery originating in the Tang Dynasty, embroidery, cloisonné, lacquer ware, batik, jade carving, just to name a few. Do you have anything in

100

mind?

A：No，not really. I think it should be something distinctively Chinese.

K：And something easy to carry.

S：Tri-colored pottery is beautiful，but it's fragile. Cloisonné is heavier and can also be damaged easily. I would suggest you buy paper cuts，embroidery and batik. They are very easy to carry.

A：Where can we find them?

S：Paper cuts are sold at the next counter，and embroidery and batik are a few counters further down.

K：Thank you.

S：Oh，madam，maybe you would like to have a look at the bamboo scrolls here. They are also easy to carry.

K：What are they?

S：They are made of bamboo pieces and painted with either birds and flowers or Chinese calligraphy.

A：Will you show us some?

S：Certainly.

A：They are beautiful. I like the one with the flowers and the phoenixes. We can hang it in our sitting room. How much is it?

S：68 yuan.

K：The price is reasonable. We'll take this one.

Notes

1. arts and crafts 手工艺品

2. embroidery *n.* 刺绣

3. cloisonné *n.* 景泰蓝瓷器 *adj.* 景泰蓝制的

4. lacquer ware 漆器

5. batik *n.* 蜡染

6. jade carving 玉雕

7. calligraphy *n.* 书法

**Dialogue Three**

Selling Silk Fabrics

(A shop assistant at the silk fabrics counter is receiving a foreign couple.)

(S＝shop assistant   G1＝guest 1   G2＝guest 2)

S：Good morning，sir and madam. Welcome to our silk fabrics counter!

G1：Good morning. I like Chinese Qipao very much. So I'd like to buy some beautiful silk fabrics to make one.

S：China is called the kingdom of silk.

G2：I couldn't stop my wife wanting to get herself dressed in silk. And I have seen many Chinese women wearing it. It's fantastic.

G1：I'm dazed at so many kinds of silk fabrics. It's difficult for me to choose one.

S：What about this one? Its touch is soft and it's 100％ pure silk.

G1：Superb! Look，the wonderful peony with purple background color. Could you tell me how many meters I need for my Qipao?

S：Would you like long or short sleeves，or the sleeveless? And what is your size?

G1：I think I like sleeveless. And I am of the medium size.

S：Eh…you need three meters. That is enough.

G1：OK. How much is that?

S：RMB 160 per meter，and the total comes to RMB 480.

G2：Here is the RMB 500.

S：Thank you. Here's the receipt. Oh，one piece of advice：wash it in lukewarm water and don't rub or wring it.

G2：Thank you for your advice. You are most helpful. Goodbye.

S：Goodbye. Have a good day.

Notes

1. silk fabric   丝织品

2. sleeveless *adj.* 无袖的

3. receipt   *n.* 发票

4. lukewarm　*adj*. 微温的，不冷不热的

5. rub or wring　揉或者拧

**Dialogue Four**

Antique Shopping

（G＝guide　　T＝tourist　　V＝vendor）

G：Have you been to this place before?

T：This is the first time. An old schoolmate told me about it.

G：Actually, this secondhand market is quite big.

T：My friend comes here every once in a while.

G：Look there, there is a vase.

T：It looks new, 20 years old at the most.

G：20 years? 200 years. Some foreigners would like to take vases home whenever they travel in Beijing, but we can come back and buy it later, otherwise we'd have to carry it. It is pretty heavy.

T：What's this cabinet made of?

V：Rose wood, real rose wood. It's been handed down in the family. It's at least four or five hundred years old.

T：Four or five hundred years old? Qing Dynasty?

Vendor：Ming Dynasty. Look at the craftsmanship. Only furniture from the Ming Dynasty is so well made.

T：How much will you pat with it for?

V：One hundred thousand.

G：That's too expensive.

V：It's a family heirloom. We could never bear to sell it before.

T：We will think about it.

V：Sure. The price is still negotiable.

G：I think it's better to buy some little things. The bigger items are too expensive, and they're hard to transport home.

T：You think smaller things cost less? Some are very pricy, too.

G：I know. Didn't you buy a super expensive pen-holder for me last time? We got so excited for nothing. It turned out to be a fake antique.

T：Don't bring that up again. You mustn't keep rubbing salt into my wounds.

G：Have a look over there. It's all small items over there.

T：The fun of coming here is treasure hunting. You get something cheaply, go home and have it authenticated, and find it's a real antique.

G：But it's not easy. You need an expert's eye.

T：Quick, look. There seems to be someone selling pen-holders.

G：Pen-holders again?

Notes

1. secondhand market　旧货市场，二手市场
   无论是在国内还是在国外，旧货市场都很火爆，只要你对你想购买的东西有所了解，而且懂得砍价（因为一开始商家都会将价位抬得很高），还是能够买到一些物美价廉的东西的。

2. How much will you pat with it for?　你要多少钱卖它啊？

3. family heirloom　传家宝

4. fake antique　赝品

5. You mustn't keep rubbing salt into my wounds.　别提我的伤心事了。

6. You need an expert's eye.　除非你是一位行家。

Part Ⅲ　Vocabulary & Useful Expressions

Ⅰ. Useful Words

specialty　*n.* 特产

distinguished　*adj.* 著名的

fit　*adj.* 适合的，健康的

kilo　*n.* 公斤，千克

change *n.* 零头，零钱

souvenir *n.* 纪念品

counter *n.* 柜台

typically *adv.* 典型地

collection *n.* 收集

medium *adj.* 中等的，适中的

traditional *adj.* 传统的

peony *n.* 牡丹

pale *adj.* 淡色的，苍白的

design *n.* 款式

exquisite *adj.* 优美的，精致的

pack *v.* 包扎，捆扎

postage *n.* 邮资，邮费

including *prep.* 包括

fabric *n.* 织品

sleeve *n.* 袖子

ginseng *n.* 人参

antique *n.* 古物，遗迹

local specialties 土特产

black tea 红茶

green tea 绿茶

come to 总计，合计

Chinese-style 中式的

Ⅱ. Useful Expressions

1. Do you find anything you like?

   你找到你喜欢的了吗?

2. What can I do for you?

   您想要些什么?

3. Can I help you?

   我能帮您吗? (您需要些什么?)

4. Are you being helped? /Are you being served?

   您需要帮忙吗?

5. Is there anybody waiting on you?

有人招呼您吗？

6. Show me that one, please.

请把那个给我看看。

7. Let me have a look at this watch.

让我看看这只表。

8. Would you show me this cup?

你能把这只杯子让我看一下吗？

9. I'm just looking, thanks.

我只是看看，谢谢。

10. I'd like to have a look if you don't mind.

如果不介意，我想看一下。

11. Could you try it on please? How is it?

请试穿看看好吗？如何？

12. Do you have any on sale?

你们有什么特卖品吗？

13. The fit isn't good.

尺寸不太合适。

14. It seems to fit well.

好像蛮合身的。

15. Can I have a size larger?

可以给我一个大一点儿的吗？

16. How much does it cost?

多少钱？

17. How much do I have to pay for it?

我要付多少钱？

18. Can you make it cheaper?

能便宜点吗？

19. How can I pay?

我要如何付钱？

20. May I write a check for you?

我能开支票吗？

Part IV   Reading Materials

Passage One

Creating a Shoppers' Paradise

Millions of foreigners and overseas Chinese visit china every year on business, for sightseeing or exchanges in the fields of economy, trade, sports, science, and culture. Many of them return home loaded with souvenirs and gifts. In fact, there cannot be many people who could manage to stay in China and not be tempted to do any shopping. China offers a dazzling range of goods from antiques, jewelry, Chinese paintings and calligraphy to chopsticks, garments, foods, Chinese patent medicines and tonics, to name just a few. In fact, shops are becoming one of the pillars that support China's tourism industry. They have been adding much to the convenience and pleasure of tourists and to the financial success of the tourism.

Arts and crafts are the main products of a scenic spot shop, which have become the favorite goods as well as eye-openers to foreign and domestic buyers. The jade carving is characterized by its distinct national style of simplicity, gracefulness and delicate lucidity. The cloisonné, which enjoys a high reputation at home and abroad, are beautiful and elegant in modeling, splendid and graceful in design and brilliant in colors. Lacquer ware, multifarious in kind and exquisite in workmanship, is noted by elegant modeling, beautiful figuration, and lustrous color. Porcelain is perhaps the greatest invention of the Chinese people. The chinaware made in Jingde Zhen—the capital of porcelain—is known to be "as white as jade, as thin as paper, as bright as mirror and as melodious as 'qing' (an ancient Chinese musical instrument)". Silk products and embroidery, exquisite in workmanship, multifarious in patterns, harmonious in color scheme, and distinctive in national style, are really good buys in China.

Many tourists are also interested in some special local crafts such as clay figurines, sandalwood fans, paper-cuttings, theatrical masks, kites, shell-carvings, etc. All in all, China is not only a country with a long history of culture and art, but also a shoppers' paradise. Shouldn't we help our tourists take home more happy memories and more keepsakes?

All this creates great opportunities for scenic spot shops. In order to meet the increasing shopping needs of the customers, the staff should not only be familiar with the goods, the price and the customers, and not only have a clean and pleasant appearance and a good command of job-procedures, but also have a correct attitude toward serving the tourists wholeheartedly. "Try to make every customer feel at home and feel the value of every coin they spend. " This is the life line of scenic spot shop, and of the whole tourism industry.

Notes

1. souvenir   *n.* 纪念品；纪念物

2. dazzling   *adj.* 眼花缭乱的，耀眼的

3. antique   *n.* 古物，古董

4. jewelry   *n.* 珠宝，首饰

5. calligraphy   *n.* 书法，书法艺术，书法作品

6. garment   *n.* 外衣

7. patent medicine   成药，专利药品，秘方药

8. tonic   *n.* 增进健康或体力的东西，补药，滋补品

9. arts and crafts   工艺

10. jade carving   玉雕

11. lucidity   *n.* 明朗，清晰，透明

12. porcelain   *n.* 瓷，瓷器

13. melodious   *adj.* 音调和谐的，有旋律的，悦耳的

14. embroidery   *n.* 刺绣，刺绣品；渲染，修饰

15. exquisite   *adj.* 优美的，高雅的，精致的

16. figurine   *n.* 小雕像

17. sandalwood   *n.* 檀香，白檀

18. paradise   *n.* 天堂

19. keepsakes   *n.* 纪念品

20. as white as jade, as thin as paper, as bright as mirror and as melodious as "qing"
    白如玉，薄如纸，明如镜，声如磬

21. multifarious in kind and exquisite in workmanship   种类丰富，风格独特

22. elegant modeling, beautiful figuration, and lustrous color   造型大方，纹饰美观，

108

色泽光润

23. clay figurines, sandalwood fans, paper-cuttings, theatrical masks, kites, shell-carvings 泥人、檀香木扇、剪纸、戏剧脸谱、风筝、贝雕

24. Try to make every customer feel at home and feel the value of every coin they spend. 我们要千方百计使每位顾客感到宾至如归，同时使顾客感到他们花的每一分钱都是值得的。

 **Passage Two**

Great Shopping Programs

China is known as a "shopping paradise" because of the huge variety of commodities, excellent quality of goods, and cheap market price. Therefore, shopping is a highlighted part of reception. In order to arrange the shopping program properly, a guide should get to know the tourist's needs in advance and make a full preparation accordingly. The related strategies are provided in a pointwise manner as follows:

First, a guide should study the tourist's shopping interests. This is an essential step in deciding a shopping strategy since the tourists come from various countries and may differ greatly in their needs for goods. The guests from the USA, the UK, and other western countries are more interested in Chinese traditional goods like silk, Chinese handcrafts, jewelry, etc, while the guests from developing countries like to buy clothes, daily commodities, electronic appliances, etc.

Second, once the needs of the tourists have been clarified, the guide should select a suitable marketplace in compliance with the needs. The guests coming from developed countries have strong purchases power and are more focused on the quality of the products, so it is proper to arrange shopping in large shopping malls or department stores. While for those guests with lower price expectations, it will be wiser to have them shop in market-style commercial areas. In some cities, there are certain famous commercial streets, like Wangfujing Pedestrian Street in Beijing, Nanjing Road in Shanghai, Beijing Road in Guangzhou and Dehua Street in Zhengzhou. These famous shopping streets are normally featured for superb collections of goods, better service, and pleasant shopping environments and, therefore, serve as good choices for shopping.

Third, the guide must have proper time management during the shopping process.

Before shopping, the guide should inform the guests of all necessary details including the duration of shopping, location of the market, payment issues, regrouping spot, and his/her contact information in case any emergencies happen. Since the tourists usually have a great zeal for buying and bargaining, time management becomes a critical task in the shopping process. Otherwise, the overtime shopping may affect the next program scheduled.

Lastly, the guide should provide assistance within his/her capacity during the process. Since most tourists will encounter language difficulties during shopping time, it will be highly appreciated by the tourists if the guide can give some language support or teach them some simple Chinese words beforehand. As the market place is normally crowded, it is a must that the guide gives clear explanations on the location of the shopping area. If possible, the guide can accompany the guests for shopping. If there are too many tourists and different shopping priorities, the guide must inform the guests of the meeting place, the way back, and relative contact details.

All in all, shopping in China is a fantastic thing to many tourists, but it can also be the most challenging job to a local guide. So please keep the safety of the tourists in mind and be alert at all times. Then a guide can help the tourists bring home both abundant Chinese products and enjoyable memories.

Notes

1. China is known as a "shopping paradise" because of the huge variety of commodities, excellent quality of goods, and cheap market price. 中国由于其商品种类繁多、质量优良且价格低廉而被称为"购物天堂"。

2. Otherwise, the overtime shopping may affect the next program scheduled. 否则，超出的购物时间会影响到下面的安排。

Part V   Skill Training

I. Matches.

a. overcoat   1. 靴子

b. sweater   2. 裤袜

c. blouse   3. 短袜

d. socks   4. 拖鞋

e. tights/pantyhose   5. 外套

f. underwear   6. 运动鞋

g. XL—extra large   7. 毛衣

h. sneakers   8. 内衣

i. sandals   9. 女用衬衫

j. boots   10. 特大号

Ⅱ. Choices.

| clarified | reception | time management | to | study | challenging |
| shopping paradise | therefore | second | with | | |

China is known as a ___1___ because of the huge variety of commodities, excellent quality of goods, and cheap market price. ___2___, shopping is a highlighted part of ___3___. First, a guide should ___4___ the tourist's shopping interests. ___5___, once the needs of the tourists have been ___6___, the guide should select a suitable marketplace in compliance ___7___ the needs. Third, the guide must have proper ___8___ during the shopping process. Lastly, the guide should provide assistance within his/her capacity during the process. All in all, shopping in China is a fantastic thing ___9___ many tourists, but it can also be the most ___10___ job to a local guide.

Ⅲ. Translate the following sentences into Chinese.

1. China is a country with a long history, splendid culture, beautiful mountains and rivers, a large number of ethnic groups and abundant tourism resources.

2. Tourism has become a fashion making people relax and pleasing to people's bodies and minds.

3. Tourism may enable people to broaden their vision and increase their knowledge.

4. In addition, the mysterious and exotic Chinese customs are attracting an increasing number of visitors both at home and abroad.

5. There is tri-colored pottery originating in the Tang Dynasty, embroidery,

cloisonné, lacquer ware, batik, jade carving, just to name a few.

Ⅳ. Translate the following sentences into English.

1. 要记住通常大多数游客的兴趣在于观光而非购物。所以要避免频繁安排购物，以免顾客厌倦和反感。

2. 为了提高市场竞争力，旅行社通常付给导游很低的报酬，这使得工资之外的小费与佣金几乎成为导游获取相对较好收入的唯一途径。

3. 在中国的许多大型商场里，一般都可以看到肯德基或麦当劳的分店。

4. 湘绣擅长表现狮虎等动物，形象刻画，真实生动，富于写实的艺术效果。

5. 中国是世界闻名的陶瓷古国，陶瓷是中国传统工艺中最重要的工艺品种之一。

Ⅴ. Situational play.

Situation 1

You are a shop assistant, you are trying to sell a camera to an interested foreign tourist in a department store. You may say as much as possible by using the following situations.

(1) Tell the prospective customer what brands of camera are available.

(2) Recommend one brand to your friends.

(3) Explain its performance.

(4) Tell the information about the price.

Situation 2

You are taking a group of Canadian tourists to visit a pedestrian mall in Guangzhou. Most of the tourists want to buy some souvenirs which are typical of the Asian Games in 2010.

(1) Recommend to the tourists what can be bought.

(2) Show them some souvenirs bearing the image of the Mascot of the Guangzhou Asian Games. (Envelops, postcards, toys, T-shirts and other accessories, etc.)

(3) Explain what the mascots represent.

(4) Introduce the models of the "Haixinsha", which is the major stadium for the games.

(5) Help them to inquire the price.

Part Ⅵ　Knowledge Expansion

购物

1. 购物习惯

许多人在国内购物的时候，都会习惯性地东拿西看，但是在国外就不可以随便触摸商品，因为这是不礼貌的行为。如果有任何需要，请服务员拿给你，如果店员对你说 "May I help you?"，不要装作没有听见，而应该友善地说 "Hello" 并回答 "I am just looking"。国内商店的店员一般会很殷勤地介绍，但是在国外，除非你有需要，否则店员只会在旁边等候你的询问，不会一直跟在你的身边。有时候会遇到店员不断推荐的情形，此时你只要说 "It is over my budget"，就不用担心对方一直不停游说了。若要询问对方穿多大码的衣服或鞋子时，可以说 "What size do you take?"。假设当顾客得知某件上衣要 8 英镑时，认为太贵了。于是她说："Do you have anything like it for less?（你们有没有像这种样式但便宜一点的?）" 表示用多少钱买某样东西时用介词 "for"，比如，I bought my new car for $20,000。

2. 相关购物场所

购物中心是 shopping mall 或者 shopping center；chain shop 是 "联营公司" 的意思；杂货店是 grocery 或者 grocery store；折扣商店和旧货店分别是 discount shop 和 second-hand shop。

百货商店（department store），一般分成很多的营业部门，你可以从中买到服装、鞋帽、电器、厨房用具、工艺品、礼品、珠宝首饰等。不同档次的百货商店出售的商品价格和质量都不一样。百货商店经常举办促销活动，在此期间选择一部分商品降价出售。多数促销活动都会在地方报纸上刊登广告。一般来说，百货商店都设在商场里面，成为那里的支柱或 "龙头店家"。

折扣商店（discount store）经营的商品与百货商店大同小异，由于它们是大批量进货（出售的商品有时也可能会过时或不再流行），又因为商店的面积比较大、造价低廉、装饰朴素，因此价格往往比百货商店要便宜一些。有些折扣商店必须交费成为成员，才能入内购物。在折扣商店里经常会有价格低廉的 "特价商品"（bargains 或 good buys）。

超级市场（supermarket），或称自选商场，在美国有时也叫做 "grocery store"。这是一种规模、面积都相当大的商店，主要销售各种副食品，同时也有选择地销售一定量的其他物品，诸如医药用品、金属器具、厨房用具、室内盆栽植物、供宠物吃的食品，有的超级市场也出售衣服。

国外有名的 "跳蚤市场"（flea market）与国内的集市贸易差不多，所售的物品有

新有旧。有时设于广场，有时在星期天借商店的走廊设摊。

3. 关于退税的方法与注意事项

出国旅游消费时，若金额达到该国退税规定，记得向店家提出欲申请退税的要求。通常店家会要求你出示护照，并给你一张收据和盖了店章的退税单。只要将这些单据收妥，在出境机场索取并填写退税申请表，连同购买物品一并办理便能申请退税。接受检查后，将已经盖章的退税申请表寄回当初购物所在的国家即可在一段时间后收到退税。

退款方式很多，填写退税申请表，便可选择以现金、支票或是汇款方式收款。如果前往旅游的国家是欧盟国家，且在该国旅行后还要继续前往其他欧盟国家，则在离开行程中的最后一个欧盟国家时办理退税。

一般来说，欲申请退税的物品，购买日期须在出国日期起三个月内，逾期则无法办理。

Chapter 7

Entertainment

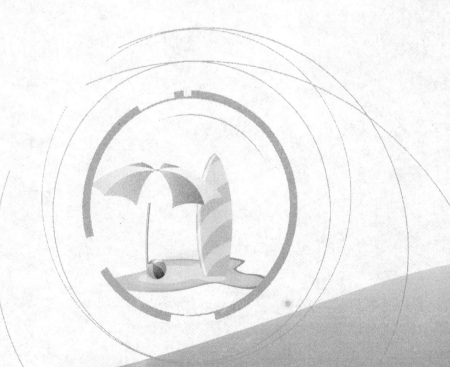

Part Ⅰ Lead-in

【本章简介】

现代旅游由"吃、住、行、游、购、娱"六要素组成，所以，安排旅游购物、旅游娱乐是旅游的两个环节。本章主要讲述导游带领游客参加娱乐活动时的相关情境，并通过延伸阅读材料介绍中国的传统艺术和文化。

【教学目标】

1. 掌握与娱乐相关的专业英文词汇及用语；
2. 学会用英文向游客介绍有关娱乐活动的信息；
3. 了解中国的传统娱乐形式；
4. 能够向外国游客介绍中国的传统文化。

【背景知识】

现代旅游不再仅限于传统的游山玩水，尤其在城市旅游过程中，游客除了欣赏美丽的自然景观和人文景观外，还愿意深入了解目的地的市井民俗和文化活动。导游可以通过适当安排游客进行形式多样、丰富多彩的娱乐活动，为国内外的游客提供全方位的服务，以满足各层次消费者的不同需求。

Part Ⅱ Situational Dialogues

Dialogue One

How do You Spend Your Spare Time?

(A and B are talking about their spare time activities.)

A：What do you usually do in your spare time?

B：It depends. When I am at school，I often read some magazines or books，or I play basketball with my classmates. If I am at home，I often watch TV. On Sundays I go shopping with my friends. What about you?

A：I like surfing the Internet at home. Sometimes my friends and I go to the concert or a disco. On Sundays，I often go swimming or take a bike ride into the country.

B：Do you like traveling?

A：Yes. I often travel with my family during the summer holiday.

B：That's good.

Notes

1. spare time   业余时间

2. depend   *v.* 依靠，取决于

3. surf   *v.* 冲浪

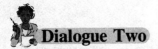 **Dialogue Two**

At the Beach

(Teddy and George are talking on the beach.)

(T＝Teddy   G＝George)

T：Wow，this is a lovely spot.

G：Yes. Isn't it nice to come here to the beach? Thousands of people come here for fun and relaxation every summer or on weekends.

T：That's an important part of people's life nowadays，especially for the people who live in big cities. After a period of hard work，they need to enjoy themselves.

G：This reminds me of the beach Florida. Local people and tourists go surrounding scenery，just like we are doing here.

T：People everywhere love water，don't they? Look at those surfers riding the waves! How exciting it is!

G：Hurry up! Let's go in!

Notes

1. at the beach　在海边
2. on weekends　在周末
3. the people who live in big cities　住在大城市的人们
4. local people　当地人
5. ride the waves　乘风破浪

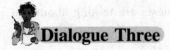Dialogue Three

I Like Beijing Opera

(A and B are talking about the traveling plan for tomorrow.)

A: Well, could you please tell me the traveling plan for tomorrow?

B: OK. We'll visit the Palace Museum in the morning. Then take a stroll in the Wangfujing Walking Street in the afternoon.

A: How about in the evening?

B: After checking in the hotel in the evening, you will have free time for leisure.

A: That's OK. Could you recommend what we can do?

B: Well, you can go to the Houhai Bar Street to have a drink. Or you can go to the Capital Theatre to watch a Beijing Opera performance.

A: I like Beijing Opera. And is it far away from our hotel?

B: Just a ten-minute walk.

A: I see. Thank you very much.

B: My pleasure.

Notes

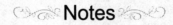

1. Beijing Opera　京剧
2. take a stroll　散步
3. Wangfujing Walking Street　王府井步行街
4. check in the hotel　入住酒店

5. have free time for leisure　有休闲时间

6. Houhai Bar Street　后海酒吧一条街

7. be far away from　离······很远

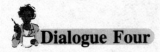
Dialogue Four

How Did You Enjoy the Play?

(After watching a performance of Beijing Opera, two guests are talking about the play.)

A: Linda, how did you enjoy the play? Did you like it very much?

B: You bet. I especially like the costume and the scenery.

A: So did I. Did you know that? Both the costume and the scenery designers are famous for their works.

B: No wonder they are so marvelous.

A: But you didn't seem to enjoy the third scene.

B: No, I didn't. I think I am still a little confused. Who's the hero of the play, the man with a monkey's face or the one with a pig's face?

A: The monkey of course. He is always the central figure. Anyhow, the one with a pig's face, who is called Zhu Bajie, always plays as a laughing stock. So many people enjoy watching his funny performance.

B: I see. Thank you very much for your explanation. I understand the play much better now. What about going to the bar and having some drinks?

A: That's a good idea. Let's go!

Notes

1. You bet.　当然

2. costume and scenery　戏装及布景

3. be famous for　因······而著名

4. no wonder　难怪

5. be confused　困惑

6. a laughing stock　笑料

Part Ⅲ   Vocabulary & Useful Expressions

Ⅰ. Useful Words

spare   *adj.* 多余的

magazine   *n.* 杂志

concert   *n.* 音乐会

ride   *v.* 骑，乘坐

spot   *n.* 地点

beach   *n.* 海滩

relaxation   *n.* 放松

nowadays   *n.* 当今，如今

period   *n.* 时期

remind   *v.* 提醒

local   *adj.* 当地的

scenery   *n.* 景色，风景

surfer   *n.* 冲浪的人

wave   *n.* 波浪

stroll   *n.* 漫步，闲逛

leisure   *n.* 闲暇，空闲

recommend   *v.* 推荐

theatre   *n.* 剧院，剧场

opera   *n.* 歌剧，戏剧

performance   *n.* 表演

costume   *n.* 戏装

designer   *n.* 设计者

marvelous   *adj.* 非凡的

confused   *adj.* 困惑的，糊涂的

figure   *n.* 人物；角色

explanation   *n.* 解释，说明

Ⅱ. Useful Expressions

1. It depends.

那要看情况而定。

2. I like surfing the Internet at home.

我喜欢在家上网。

3. I often travel with my family during the summer holiday.

我经常在暑假和家人一起去旅游。

4. Isn't it nice to come here to the beach?

来到海滩真好啊!

5. That's an important part of people's life nowadays，especially for the people who live in big cities.

现在，它对人们的生活非常重要，尤其是对那些住在大城市的人。

6. Then take a stroll in the Wangfujing Walking Street in the afternoon.

然后下午我们到王府井步行街玩。

7. Just a ten-minute walk.

步行十分钟就到了。

8. Both the costume and the scenery designers are famous for their works.

布景和戏装都是由名家设计的。

9. He is always the central figure.

他通常都是主角。

10. Thank you very much for your explanation.

非常感谢您的解说。

Part Ⅳ   Reading Materials

**Passage One**

Acrobatic Arts

The Chinese acrobatics have come a long way. They remain as one of the most popular art forms in China and have gone through extensive evolution and development to reach their current level and fame. The art has actually existed for more than two thousand years but was never performed before liberation as it was looked down on by the feudal class. Only after 1949 did the people's government make intense efforts to foster and develop national arts and only then did the Chinese acrobatics gain a new life. The art has not only made great improvement in its contents and skills but also achieved in setting up a designing and directing system. This movement aimed to create graceful images, harmonious musical accompaniment, and good supporting effects of costumes, props and lighting.

During the arduous course of development, the Chinese acrobatics art managed to form its own style. The ancient acrobatics originated from the people's lives and were closely linked to their daily living and productive labor. Instruments of labor and everyday articles such as tridents, wicker rings, tables, chairs, jars, plates and bowls were used in the performances. Challenging acts were developed— "Flying Trident", "Balancing Chairs", "Trick with Jars", "Hoop-Diving" and "Traditional Conjuring" are all equally intriguing performances not to be missed. In addition, there are Wushu, Diabolo Skills and the famous Lion Dance, all conceived from folk sports and games.

Notes

1. acrobatics *n.* 杂技
2. extensive *adj.* 广泛的，大量的
3. evolution *n.* 演变，进化
4. fame *n.* 名声，名气
5. only then 直到那时
6. content *n.* 内容
7. achieve *v.* 达到，完成
8. aim to 以……为目标
9. graceful *adj.* 优美的
10. harmonious *adj.* 和谐的，悦耳的
11. trident *n.* 三叉戟
12. wicker *adj.* 柳条编织的
13. jar *n.* 罐子
14. conjuring *n.* 魔术
15. intriguing *n.* 有趣的，迷人的
16. Diabolo *n.* 空竹

17. conceive v. 构思

 **Passage Two**

Beijing Opera

Beijing Opera is an integrated performing art on the Chinese stage. It has four areas of performance: singing, dialogue, acting and acrobatic combat. Beijing Opera is developed from local opera in Anhui and Hubei provinces. It has now become the most influential and popular opera in China. Of the many different characters in Beijing Opera, there are four main ones. They are the male lead, the female lead, the painted face and the clown. The male lead plays the role of an ordinary man; the female lead plays that of a woman; the painted face represents men with distinctly different looks and characters; and the clown represents humorous or evil men. Beijing Opera combines many art forms. Apart from singing and recitation, it includes traditional Chinese music, poetry, dancing, pantomime, elaborate costumes and make-up, acrobatic and martial arts. Although the stage settings are much simpler than that in Western Operas, they are usually drawn from Chinese art, so painting also plays a part. Beijing Opera has a history of about 200 years. Until the beginning of this century, all the operatic roles were taken by men with female impersonator, playing the part of women. The best known of these was Mei Lanfang. He toured several countries in order to introduce Beijing Opera to foreign audiences. Now men don't play female parts any more. But all actors and actresses have to be very versatile. Not only must they be able to sing, act and recite poetry, but also they need to be skilled in martial arts and gestures. It takes a performer from a professional Beijing Opera troupe 12 years of basic training before he or she can go on stage.

Notes

1. an integrated performing art 综合表演艺术
2. singing, dialogue, acting and acrobatic combat 唱、念、坐、打
3. the male lead, the female lead, the painted face and the clown 生、旦、

净、丑

4. play the role of   扮演……的角色

5. apart from...   除了……

6. pantomime   *n.* 哑剧

7. elaborate costumes and make up   精致的道具和化妆

8. martial arts   武术

9. be drawn from   吸取了

10. female impersonator   男扮女装

11. versatile   *adj.* 多才多艺的；多功能的

12. gesture   *n.* 架势

Part Ⅴ   Skill Training

Ⅰ. Matches.

a. costume	1. free time
b. spare time	2. waves breaking on the shore
c. confuse	3. be contingent (something that is elided)
d. surf	4. an area of sand sloping down to the water of a sea or lake
e. performance	5. freedom from activity (work or strain or responsibility)
f. depend	6. the appearance of a place
g. beach	7. the attire worn in a play or at a fancy dress ball
h. scenery	8. mistaken one thing for another
i. relaxation	9. a diagram or picture illustrating textual material
j. figure	10. a dramatic or musical entertainment

Ⅱ. Choices.

be famous for	beach	figure	local	performance
surf	designer	explanation	leisure	scenery

1. Beidaihe _____ its sand beach.

2. If so，science might have an _____.

3. I draw the flowers in spring，the _____ in summer.

4. The _____ was cancelled because of the bad weather.

5. I _____ the Internet 2 hours a day.

6. He was a _____ from another age.

7. Her sister is a fashion _____.

8. Perhaps you could find the information in the _____ newspaper.

9. I also like _____ of Swiss.

10. I would travel around the world if I were rich and had a lot of _____.

Ⅲ. Translate the following expressions into Chinese.

1. I can't help getting excited as soon as I get on my horse.

2. What is your city famous for，silk or chinaware?

3. I often climb the mountains with my friends on weekend.

4. The shopping center is not far away from your hotel.

5. The two sisters are very much alike. I was confused.

Ⅳ. Translate the Chinese in brackets into English.

1. What do you often do _____（在业余时间）?

2. We can _____（享受生活）better when we are healthy.

3. The details will _____（取决于）negotiation with the company.

4. _____（难怪）competition to secure a job is so intense.

5. During the weekend，we often went to _____（散步）.

Ⅴ. Situational play.

Situation 1

A and B are vocational school classmates. They haven't met for a long time. Now they are talking about what they do in their spare time. A is still fond of music and garden-keeping. B has just come back from abroad, who has learnt how to play football and ski. Make a dialogue between them.

Situation 2

You are a disco worker. A foreign guest comes to get some information about your disco. Make a dialogue.

Part VI Knowledge Expansion

大型实景演出

大型实景演出是一个以真山真水为演出舞台、以当地文化和民俗为主要内容、以演艺界和商业界大师为创作团队的独特的文化模式，是中国人的独创，是中国旅游业向人文旅游、文化旅游转型下的特殊产物。

大型桂林山水实景演出《印象·刘三姐》，由我国著名导演张艺谋等出任总导演，历时三年半努力制作而成。它集漓江山水风情、广西少数民族文化及中国精英艺术家创作之大成，是全世界第一部全新概念的"山水实景演出"。

方圆两公里的阳朔书童山段漓江水域，十二座背景山峰，广袤无际的天穹，构成迄今世界上最大的山水剧场。传统演出是在剧院有限的空间里进行的，这场演出则以自然造化为实景舞台，放眼望去，漓江的水、桂林的山，化为中心舞台，给人宽广的视野和超然的感受。山峰的隐现、水镜的倒影、烟雨的点缀、竹林的轻吟随时都会进入演出，成为美妙的插曲。演出利用晴、烟、雨、雾、春、夏、秋、冬不同的自然气候，创造出无穷的神奇魅力，使那里的演出每场都是新的。

中国·漓江山水剧场（原"刘三姐歌圩"）坐落在漓江与阳朔田家河交汇处，占地面积近 100 亩，几乎全部被绿色覆盖，里面种植有茶树、凤尾竹等，加上所植草皮，绿化率达到 90% 以上。其中，灯光、音响系统均采用隐蔽式设计，与环境融为一体，水上舞台全部采用竹排搭建，不演出时可以全部拆散、隐蔽，对漓江水体及河床不造成影响。演出以"印象·刘三姐"为主题，将刘三姐留给人们的印象深刻的经典山歌与民族风情、漓江渔火等元素创新组合，不着痕迹地融入山水，还原于自然，成功诠释了人与自然的和谐关系，创造出天人合一的境界。

观众席由绿色梯田造型构成，180 度全景视觉，可观赏江上两公里范围的景物及演出。演员阵容强大，由 600 多名经过特殊训练的演员构成；演出服装多姿多彩，根据不同的场景选用了壮族、瑶族、苗族等不同少数民族的服装；整个演出时间约 90 分钟。目前已申报了两项吉尼斯纪录：一是世界上最大的鼓楼群；二是世界上最大的山水实景剧场。

Chapter 8

Sightseeing

Part I Lead-in

【本章简介】

本章主要介绍旅游过程中最基本的一项活动内容——观光，如观赏异国异地的风景名胜、人文古迹、城市美景及了解当地的风土人情等。读者通过对本章的学习，将进一步感受到观光在人们开阔眼界、增长见识、陶冶性情、鉴赏大自然造化之美等方面的重要作用。

【教学目标】

1. 掌握有关观光旅游的词汇和短语；
2. 掌握观光旅游的基本英语对话；
3. 提高与观光消费者的沟通交往能力。

【背景知识】

随着社会的发展进步，团体旅游和旅行社的兴起和发展，旅游活动变得方便轻松，真正成为一种享受。目前已进入大众旅游时代，旅游的主要目的是观光娱乐、消遣休闲。旅游者通过观光游览可达到暂时改变常居环境、开阔眼界、陶冶情操、欣赏自然之美、享受现代化生活的情趣等多方面的需求和目的。这种基本的旅游方式，在今后一定时期内仍将继续占据重要地位。在不少国家，"观光"（sightseeing）一词即游览或旅游的同义词，观光者（sightseer）即旅游者。

Part II Situational Dialogues

Dialogue One

(T＝Tom   M＝Mary)

T：So, what do you want to do tomorrow?

M：Well, let's look at this city guide here. Okay, uh, here's something interest-

ing. Oh! Why don't we first visit the art museum in the morning?

T：Okay. I like that idea. And where do you want to have lunch?

M：How about going to an Indian restaurant? Hum…The guide recommends one downtown a few blocks from the museum.

T：That sounds great. After that, what do you think about visiting the zoo? Oh…umm…well…Well, it says here that there are some unique animals not found anywhere else.

M：Well, to tell you the truth, I'm not really interested in going there.

T：Really?

M：Yeah. Why don't we go shopping instead? There are supposed to be some really nice places to pick up souvenirs.

T：Nah, I don't think that's a good idea. We only have few traveler's checks left, and I only have fifty dollars left in cash.

M：No problem. We can use your credit card to pay for my new clothes.

T：Oh, no. I remember the last time you used my credit card for your purchases.

M：Oh, well. Let's take the subway down to the seashore and walk along the beach.

T：Now that sounds like a wonderful plan.

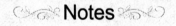

Notes

1. recommend   *v.* 推荐

2. block   *n.* 街区

3. zoo   *n.* 动物园

4. be supposed to   应该

5. souvenir   *n.* 纪念品

6. subway   *n.* 地铁

7. seashore   *n.* 海岸，海滨

Dialogue Two

A：There are so many places to go on our sightseeing trip that I am having trouble narrowing it down.

B：Let's figure out what to do before lunch and later figure out what to do in the afternoon.

A：I heard that the local beach is a place that can't be missed.

B：That would be a relaxing way to begin our morning. It would be good to get out in the sun.

A：The Natural History Museum is close by, isn't it?

B：Of course. That museum is supposed to be fantastic!

A：Do you have any suggestions as to where we could go in the afternoon?

B：We could check out the local amusement park.

A：We could eat dinner and watch the sun go down at that restaurant by the park.

B：That could really end up being a great day!

Notes

1. narrow down   减少/缩小范围
2. figure out   算出，理解，决定
3. fantastic   *adj*. 了不起的，很棒的
4. amusement   *n*. 娱乐，消遣

Dialogue Three

(C＝clerk   H＝Hans)

C：Hello.

H：Hello.

C：Can I help you?

H：Well，I want to charter a car for sightseeing. Can you tell me the price?

C：The price list and service details are in the booklet. Please take a look at it.

H：Can you tell me some scenic spots that are worth a visit?

C：Of course，there are many scenic spots，such as the Temple of Heaven，the Forbidden City，the Great Wall and more.

H：Moreover，I need a guide who can speak German. Can you arrange for one to accompany me?

C：I am afraid only English speaking guides are available.

H：All right. Then I will make the reservation without a guide for the following week.

133

Notes

1. charter   *v.* 包租，租用
2. booklet   *n.* 小册子
3. scenic spot   景点
4. arrange   *v.* 安排
5. accompany   *v.* 陪伴
6. available   *adj.* 可利用的

Dialogue Four

A：Hi! I need some sightseeing advice.

B：That's what I'm here for, sir. Every good hotel has a concierge like me.

A：I don't travel a lot. What exactly is a concierge?

B：A concierge helps visitors like you find great places to visit, shop and eat.

A：That's great! So tell me, where should I go first?

B：I'd suggest that you start at the Statue of Liberty.

A：You know, I've already been there. Can you suggest another place?

B：Maybe. Tell me what you like to do in your spare time.

A：When I have some free time, I often spend it running or at museums.

B：Well, have you ever been to either Central Park or the Museum of Modern Art?

A：No, but I sure would like to.

B：Central Park is great for just about everything outdoors. Then you can visit the Museum of Modern Art.

A：Both places sound great. I'll try to do that today.

B：Enjoy the views at both places.

Notes

1. concierge   *n.* 看门人；旅馆服务台职员
2. statue   *n.* 雕塑

3. liberty   *n.* 自由

4. outdoors   *adv.* 在户外

Part Ⅲ   Vocabulary & Useful Expressions

Ⅰ. Useful Words

landscape   *n.*   风景

cavern   *n.*   岩洞

stalagmite   *n.*   石笋

concessions   *n.*   优惠价格，（票价）优惠

tourist information   观光服务处

one-day trip/sightseeing   一日游

half-day trip   半日游

tourist spot   观光胜地

famous spot   名胜

historic site   古迹

scenic spots and historical sites   名胜古迹

botanical garden   植物园

China National Tourism Administration   中国国家旅游局

international travel service   国际旅行社

tourism company   旅游公司

spring outing   春游

autumn outing/fall excursion   秋游

overseas tour   境外旅游

licensed tourist guide   持证导游

guide interpreter   导游翻译

student guide   实习导游

tourist brochure   导游手册

natural scenery   自然景观

places of cultural and historical interest   人文景观

summer resort   避暑胜地

holiday resort　度假胜地

mountain resort　避暑山庄

ancient architectural complex　古建筑群

water-eroded cave　溶洞

limestone cave　石灰石洞

tour operators　旅游组织者

Ⅱ. Useful Expressions

1. Access all day.

   全天开放。

2. Admission is free.

   不收门票。

3. Advanced booking is essential to avoid disappointment.

   提前预订，以免错过。

4. Child reductions.

   儿童优惠。

5. One-day trip to...

   ……一日游。

6. Discounts available for pre-booked groups.

   团体提前预订优惠。

7. Fine views of London.

   伦敦美景。

8. For more detailed information please call.

   欲知详情，请打电话。

9. Free children admission with full paying adult.

   卖成人票，儿童免票。

10. Free children ticket with this leaflet.

    持本广告儿童免票。

11. Free entry for all.

    向所有人开放。

12. Free entry to over 60 attractions.

    免费到 60 多个景点旅游。

13. Shopping offers.

    提供购物机会。

14. Sights of London.
    伦敦风光。

15. Sightseeing at its best!
    观光游览最佳季节。

16. Tours take up to two hours.
    游程两个小时。

17. Tours are held throughout the day.
    旅游活动全天进行。

18. Tours have live English commentary.
    游览配有现场英语解说。

Part Ⅳ   Reading Materials

Passage One

Sightseeing in London

Today I will talk about the most famous tourist attraction in London. For every foreigner traveling in London, no one will miss this best place for sightseeing. As a sign of London and a symbol of England, it is the largest four-faced chiming clock and the third-tallest free-standing clock tower in the world. People kindly called it Big Ben.

The clock was built on 10 April, 1858, until now it has been 154 years old. Big Ben weighs 13.5 tons which is huge and gorgeous. It is located in the north of Houses of Parliament, giving a deep impression on visitors.

Clock Tower is an important place of new year celebrations in the United Kingdom, with radio and TV stations tuning to its sound of the clock ringing to welcome the start of the year. It can ring on time every 15 minutes to tell people the correct time.

The clock's movement is famous for its reliability. It kept hard working even during World War Ⅱ. It also can normally work. If you stay here, you could adjust time

on your mobile phone or watch.

Of course, Clock Tower is a significant element in popular culture. Walking down the street, you can see the pictures of Big Ben in every souvenir. Most travelers who come to sightsee in London will take photos with Big Ben. When he comes back home to show the photos with Big Ben to his friends, it proves that he has traveled in London. Big Ben was the Iconic London Film Location. In many films, you can see Big Ben as the background. A survey of 2,000 people found that Big Ben was the most popular landmark in the United Kingdom.

London is a very attractive city and there are a lot of famous tourist attractions. Near the Clock Tower, you can see the London eye. Along the River Thames, you can take ship to Tower Bridge and visit the British museum. If your journey is not short, you can spend more time there. Next, welcome Saharan to introduce the delicious food in London.

Notes

1. parliament   *n.* 国会
2. reliability   *n.* 可信度
3. adjust   *v.* 调整
4. significant   *adj.* 有意义的，重要的

Passage Two

If you have ever dreamt of traveling by camel through golden deserts or wandering through mysterious ancient cities, then the chance may now be open to you.

On October 15, China agreed to the opening of tourist routes to Jordan in the western Asia. So, we can find lots of ancient buildings of Petra in Jordan. The country has one of the Middle East's greatest historical and architectural treasures—the ancient rose-colored city of Petra. Located deep within a narrow desert gorge, Petra's most striking sights are the towering temples carved into the cliff faces. They are unlike anything you have ever seen. The unique scenery attracted the attention of

Hollywood filmmakers, who shot one of the "Indiana Jones" films at the ancient site.

❧ Notes ❧

1. mysterious   *adj.* 神秘的
2. Jordan   *n.* 约旦
3. architectural   *adj.* 建筑的
4. gorge   *n.* 峡谷
5. carve   *v.* 雕刻
6. cliff   *n.* 悬崖

| Part Ⅴ   Skill Training

Ⅰ. **Matches.**

a. adjust   1. 推荐
b. delicious   2. 纪念品
c. reliability   3. 地铁
d. accompany   4. 自由
e. amusement   5. 预订
f. liberty   6. 陪伴
g. subway   7. 娱乐，消遣
h. reservation   8. 可信度
i. recommend   9. 调整
j. souvenir   10. 美味的

Ⅱ. **Choices.**

interesting to along with weather fogs of as through one hardly

London is a wonderful city. It is very large. The River Thames（泰晤士河）runs
___1___ the city from west ___2___ the east. So the city has two parts: the South and the

North. In the North are important buildings, shops and __3__ places.

The __4__ in London is good. In winter, it is not very cold and in summer it is not very hot because the city is near the sea. People say that London is a foggy city and it often rains. It is true.

Last year when I was in London, I met __5__ of the thickest __6__ in years. You could __7__ see your hand in front __8__ your face. Cars and buses moved __9__ their lights on when evening fell, the weather got even worse. The fog was as thick __10__ milk. So the buses and cars stopped.

Ⅲ. Translate the following sentences into Chinese.

1. Wear comfortable clothes so that you don't need to worry about your clothes getting dirty while sightseeing.

2. Are you sure you can get a vacation from work?

3. My visa has already been approved.

4. What is the most popular tourist attraction here?

5. The best way to go sightseeing is usually alone so that you can enjoy all the views without people rushing you.

Ⅳ. Translate the following sentences into English.

1. 在拂晓和黄昏的时候，往往能欣赏到美丽的景色。

2. 我更喜欢去那些人不是太多的地方，体验那里的风土人情，而不是去那些著名的景点。

3. 如果你参观中国的一些历史遗址，一定要先了解一下它们的背景知识。

4. 我喜欢旅游，喜欢到美丽的风景区摄影。

5. 有些地方不容错过，有些则可以忽略。

Ⅴ. Situational play.

Situation 1

You plan to go sightseeing next week. In order to get better preparation, you go to a travel agency to consult. A clerk meets you.

Situation 2

Suppose you want to rent a car on National Day for traveling. Tom is your friend who is an experienced guide. So, you phone him for detailed information.

Part VI   Knowledge Expansion

国外观光旅游常见警示牌与标志汇总 （Notices and Signs）

Exact Fare Only	请自备零钱
Do Not Stand In Step Well	请勿站在门口
Do Not Block	请往里面走
In the Plane	飞机内
No Smoking	禁止吸烟
Fasten Seat Belts	请系安全带
Hotels	饭店
Entrance	入口
Exit/Way Out	出口
Registration /Front Desk	柜台
Cashier	付费处
Cloakroom	行李保管处
Annex	建筑物增建的部分
Mezzanine	夹层楼面
Gentlemen/Men	男厕所
Ladies/Women	女厕所
Employees Only	闲人免进
Do Not Disturb	请勿打扰
Caution	注意
Mind Your Step	注意脚下
Watch Your Head	注意头顶
Danger	危险
Keep Out/No Admittance/No Entrance	禁止入内
Out Of Order	故障
Not In Use	停止使用
Wet Paint	油漆未干
Keep Off Grass	请勿践踏草坪
No Parking/No Standing	禁止停车
Admission Free	免费入场

To Admit One	只限一人
Route/This Way	遵循路线
First Aid	急救室

To Admit One 只限一人
House Full 客满
Sold out 售完
Photographs Prohibited 禁止摄影
No Flashes 禁止闪光灯
Route/This Way 遵循路线
First Aid 急救室
Stores and Administrative Measures 商店与公共设施
Open 正在营业
Closed 停止营业
Closed Sundays 星期日休假
Business As Usual 照常营业
Duty Free Shop 免税商店
For Sale 出售
For Rent 出租
Do Not Touch 请勿触摸
Free 请自行取阅
Not For Sale 非卖品
Sample 样品
Reserved 已预约

Chapter 9

Complaints

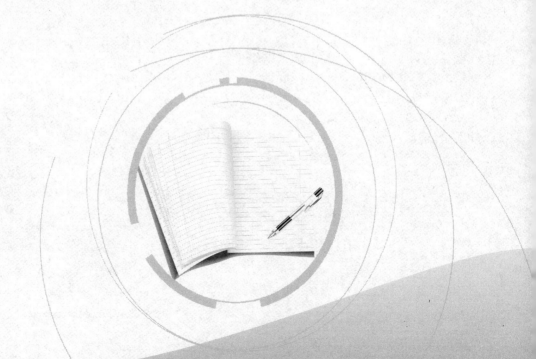

Part I   Lead-in

【本章简介】

本章主要讲述旅游过程中，如何应对游客的抱怨和投诉。旅行社和旅游服务人员总想尽力提供最好的服务，但是在旅游高峰期和天气异常等特殊情况下，游客的抱怨和投诉会增加。通过本章内容的学习，读者学会处理各种类型的投诉。

【教学目标】

1. 掌握旅游过程中游客抱怨和投诉的类型；
2. 熟悉抱怨和投诉的相关英语表达；
3. 学会如何回复游客的抱怨与投诉；
4. 学会正确处理和解决游客的抱怨与投诉。

【背景知识】

旅游投诉是指游客、海外旅行商、国内旅游经营者为维护自身和他人的旅游合法权益，对损害其合法权益的旅游经营者和有关服务单位，以书面或口头形式向旅游行政管理部门提出投诉，请求处理的行为。游客旅游心情的好坏会直接影响到整个游程的成败。旅游服务人员应耐心地倾听游客的抱怨和投诉，积极采取措施解决游客提出的问题，使游客心情愉悦地完成旅程。

Part II   Situational Dialogues

Dialogue One

(David is a very picky man with a short temper. Today he has come all the way to

a renowned restaurant to try some chef's specialties. But to his disappointment, the steak he orders is not fresh. When he asks for his bill, a waiter comes to him.)

(W＝waiter   D＝David)

W：Is everything to your satisfaction?

D：No, the steak was recommended, but it is not very fresh.

W：Oh, sorry to hear that. This is quite unusual as we have fresh steak from the market every day. I will look into the matter.

D：So what? It is not fresh and I am not happy about it.

W：I am sorry, sir. Do you wish to try something else? That would be on the house, of course.

D：No, I don't want to try anything else and find it is not fresh again! This is very annoying.

W：Please be assured that we will look into the matter. Our chef is very particular. I am sure everything will meet your expectations next time you come.

D：Don't be so sure of it yet.

W：I have every confidence in our chef. Just give us another chance, you will find this restaurant really lives up to its name.

D：All right, I will come again.

W：Thank you very much, sir.

Notes

1. a very picky man   非常挑剔的人

2. a short temper   急脾气

3. renowned   有名的，有声望的，享有盛誉的

4. That would be on the house.   那些都是本店的特色佳肴。

5. meet your expectations   达到您的预期

**Dialogue Two**

Missing Luggage

(Mr. Smith is a tourist. Amy is a tour guide.)

(A＝Amy   S＝Mr. Smith   Z＝Mr. Zhang)

S: Excuse me, is this all the luggage?

A: Yes, I think so.

S: My luggage seems to be missing.

A: How many pieces do you have?

S: Two. A large red hard-cover one and a small dark blue one; both have wheels.

A: Could I see your luggage claim checks?

S: Yes, here you are.

A: May I have your full name?

S: John Smith.

A: I have it. Just a moment and I will check it out for you.

(After a few minutes.)

A: Well, Mr. Smith, your luggage seems to have been misplaced.

S: What am I supposed to do? They have all my things.

A: I am terribly sorry. We will get in touch with the airline and try our best to get them back as soon as possible. Please find out this claim form with your check number.

S: OK. What will happen if you can't find them?

A: Well, Mr. Smith, I do not work for the airline. Let me get a representative from the airline to speak with you. He or she can answer your questions more completely.

S: My vacation is ruined. I am sure I will never see my luggage again.

A: Please, Mr. Smith, let's talk to an airline official.

(After five minutes.)

A: Here is Mr. Zhang. He is in charge of commercial luggage for this airport.

S: Well, Mr. Zhang, what are you doing about my bags?

Z: Mr. Smith, I am very sorry for this inconvenience. We are working to correct this mistake immediately.

S: I want my things by tomorrow morning at 7 or I will write to the tour company and the airline.

Z: Mr. Smith, we will need a little more time than that, because we should first locate your luggage tonight. It will take more time to get it here.

S: Well, I am not leaving my hotel room until I have my clothes.

A: Mr. Smith, let me talk to the hotel. I think we can arrange to have your clothes washed tonight while you sleep so you can enjoy tomorrow's sightseeing.

S：What happens if you can't find my bags?

Z：Let me first gather the information we have and talk to you tomorrow, when we know more.

A：Please, Mr. Smith, let's proceed to the hotel, where you can rest after your journey and enjoy a fine Chinese meal.

S：OK, that sounds good.

Notes

1. How many pieces do you have?　您一共有几件行李？
2. luggage claim checks　行李票据
3. representative　负责人，代表
4. proceed to　前往

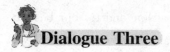

An Angry Tourist

(Mr. Wang is a local tour guide. Mr. Smith is a tourist.)

(W＝Mr. Wang　　S＝Mr. Smith)

W：You asked to see me, Mr. Smith?

S：I certainly did. I am not at all happy.

W：What seems to be the problem, Mr. Smith? How can I help you?

S：You can help me by getting my bathroom right. It is in an absolutely terrible condition. When I tried the shower, no water came out at all. I am wondering why you put me in such a room. You should have known its condition before we arrived.

W：Oh, dear, I am sorry to hear that. There has been a misunderstanding. I will have it fixed immediately.

S：That's not all. There is no soap, towels and toilet paper.

W：I apologize for this, Mr. Smith. The hotel is rather short-staffed at present. The housekeeping staff should have checked your room. I will attend to it as soon as possible.

S：Don't bother, Mr. Wang, I am not happy with this room for some other reasons too. Look, it isn't a twin room, but a double room with one double bed for two people.

How can Mr. White and I sleep in one bed? Besides, this room faces the street. It is rather noisy. Could you change it to a quiet room? It doesn't have to be on the same floor.

W: No problem. Mr. Smith, I will talk to the receptionist.

(After contacting the front office.)

W: Well, Mr. Smith, could you move to the adjacent room, that is Room 401? In the meantime, I will send up a porter to help you with your luggage, whenever you are ready to move out.

S: Thank you for your patience. Mr. Wang. You are really very helpful. We are lucky to have you as our local guide.

W: It is my pleasure, Mr. Smith. Just try to get hold of me whenever you need my help.

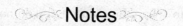

Notes

1. rather short-staffed　人手短缺，人员紧张
2. housekeeping staff　客房服务人员
3. twin room　双人间（两张单人床）
4. double room　双人间（一张双人床）
5. porter　*n.* 门童，行李员
6. local guide　地接导游

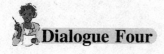

Dialogue Four

A Demanding Tourist

(Li is a tour guide. Mrs. DuPont is a tourist.)

(L=Li　　D=Mrs. DuPont)

L: Good morning, Mrs. DuPont. Is everything all right?

D: No, it's not. Someone stole some of my valuables—two rings and a gold watch.

L: I am very sorry to hear that, madam. Where were they?

D: In my room, the door was locked. It can only be one of the staff, I want my things back and fast.

L: Well, I can certainly understand that you are upset about losing them and I will do all I can to help. If they really are missing, it's a matter for the police.

D: What do you mean if they are missing? I told you they were.

L: Yes, madam. But first I'll have one of the housekeeping staff look through your room in case they are still there.

D: I don't want anyone from the staff in my room! They are the ones who have taken my belongings so they certainly will not find my jewelry.

L: Now Mrs. DuPont, why do you think the staff robbed you?

D: Well, they are the only people who can enter the rooms freely.

L: Exactly, so don't you think the hotel would be very careful with whom they entrust this freedom? Also, the hotel knows how important it is to protect its reputation if it is to have a successful business. Besides, the staff do not want to lose their jobs and face prosecution. They would be the first to be suspected.

D: Yes. That will do to start. But what if you do not find my things?

L: Then we will tell the duty manager so he can work to see if the hotel can find your belongings. Perhaps you have left them somewhere else? If not, I am sure the management will talk with the housekeeping staff and others who have access to your room. The police will also be notified.

D: That sounds like a good plan.

L: Let's start now. This way, hopefully we can find your things and you can get back to enjoy your vacation in China.

D: You're right, Li.

❧ Notes ❧

1. valuable(s)　　*n.* 贵重物品
2. belonging(s)　　*n.* 私有财产, 个人物品

| Part Ⅲ　Vocabulary & Useful Expressions

Ⅰ. Useful Words

bear/tolerate　*v.*　　忍受

awful　*adj.*　　糟糕的

inconceivable　*adj.*　　不可思议的

incident/matter　*n.*　事件

investigate　*v.*　调查

disturbance　*n.*　干扰，打扰

nuisance　*n.*　麻烦事

remedy　*v.*　补救

solve　*v.*　解决

recurrence　*n.*　再次发生

complain against somebody about something　投诉某人关于某事

dissatisfaction with　不满于……

put up with　忍受

poor service　糟糕的服务

out of one's expectation　令某人大失所望

look into/go into　调查

sanitary situation　卫生条件

bad manners　不礼貌

Ⅱ. Useful Expressions

1. I am writing to you to complain about…

   我写信来向你投诉……

2. I am writing to express my dissatisfaction with…

   我写信来表达我对……的不满。

3. There are some problems with the flat that I wish to bring to attention. For one thing，there is…For another…

   这间公寓存在一些问题，我希望能引起重视。一方面是……，另一方面是……

4. I can hardly bear /tolerate /put up with it any more…

   我再也无法忍受……

5. I hope that the authorities concerned will consider my suggestions and improve the situation as best as they can.

   我希望相关部门能考虑我的建议，并尽最大的努力改善这种状况。

6. I sincerely hope that it will review its management system，with the view to providing better service to the public.

   我由衷地希望能够从为顾客提供更好的服务的角度出发，仔细研究管理制度。

7. We trust that you will now consider this matter seriously and make an effort to prevent the recurrence of this kind.

我们相信，您会认真对待此事，并会为避免此类事件再次发生而做出努力。

8. We will appreciate your willingness to make up for the loss.

我们很感谢您愿意为损失做出补偿。

Part Ⅳ   Reading Materials

How to Deal with the Complaints?

A Six-step Procedure for Handling Guest's Complaints

1. When a guest addresses a complaint, actively listen with sincere interest.

2. Express a desire to help, and ask the guest for more information, if needed.

3. State back to the guest what you think of his or her complaint is to check on understanding.

4. Offer one or more solutions to the guest.

5. If the guest is happy with a solution, act on it quickly. If the guest is not happy with any of the solutions, or you do not have the authority to resolve the matter satisfactorily, get the manager.

6. Follow up with the guest to make sure he is satisfied.

Some Don'ts and Do's for Handling Complaints

◆ Don'ts

1. Blame anyone. This does not solve the problem and it has negative effects on the restaurant and you.

2. Argue. Nobody ever wins an argument with the guest. Keep in mind that the guest may not be right, but he or she is never wrong.

3. Get defensive. If you remember not to talk a guest's comments personally, you won't get defensive.

◆ Do's

1. Emphasize resolving the problem instead of finding someone to blame.

2. Act positively and use positive language. For example, use the word "concern" instead of "problem".

3. Respond quickly.

4. Respect the guest and treat him or her accordingly.

5. Speak to your manager when you doubt about what to do.

How to Deal with Telephone Complaints

There is another common form of complaint, which not only can be generally used for informal minor complaints, but can also be used by a highly dissatisfied customer who does not wish to write. Phone complaints allow you to look into a problem, but do not usually give you as much time to solve it as a letter or E-mail. It can be more difficult to deal with a telephone complaint than one made in person by a customer. People can be very angry and abusive in a telephone conversation, as they cannot see what is happening or the impact their words are having on the receiver of the call. In order to avoid further irritating the customer should

1. adopt an understanding tone of voice;

2. use active listening responses and try to deal with the caller's feeling before attempting to solve the problem;

3. handle the call efficiently;

4. transfer the call to another person only after explaining the situation to him.

As with face-to-face complaints, it is important to follow through on any agreed action and to consider whether any action is required to stop a similar problem occurring again.

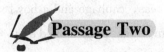

Passage Two

The Holiday from Hell

Last year, Mark and Rosa saved up money and booked their dream holiday in the Caribbean. Let us read what the holiday brochure said: luxurious hotel close to beautiful sandy beach; three swimming pools, tennis, golf and water sports; three beach bars and first-class restaurant; average temperatures 28℃ to 30℃; average hours of sunshine per day 8 to 9 hours; flying time eight and a half hours; airport fifteen mi-

nutes by bus from the hotel.

Unfortunately, the holiday was awful. In fact, Mark and Rosa appeared on a program called Holiday in Hell to describe it. Mark and Rosa decided to have a really good holiday—a dream holiday in the Caribbean, because they had always wanted to go there. So they saved up money for months and months, and booked this holiday in a place called San Antonio. It cost over a thousand pounds each, but they wanted to do something really special, so they booked it for two weeks in May. They were flying from Gatwick airport, and the flight was overnight... leaving Gatwick late at night, and arriving in San Antonio the next morning. But when they arrived at the airport, travel agency told them that because of bad weather in the Caribbean, the flight was delayed until the next morning. So they had to spend the night at the airport sleeping on the floor and they finally got on the plane the next morning twelve hours late. That was just the beginning. On the plane, the tour guide told them that the bad weather over the Caribbean was actually a hurricane and none of them could fly to San Antonio. They had to go to the capital city instead, and stayed in a hotel there for a night until the hurricane passed. Anyway they weren't too worried, thought just one night... and the tour guide told them that they were going to a five-star hotel, next to the beach, so they were quite happy at that point...

What a joke. They said it was a five-star hotel, Mark and Rosa wouldn't give it one star. It was just awful...it was an awful building , it was next to the sea, but it wasn't a beach, just a few rocks and the sea was so dirty, the sea was all polluted and brown. Then there was the food. They will never forget it, expecting to have the usual things you should in hotels, coffee, bread and fruit, and they were very surprised instead to see lots of different types of vegetables—carrots, peas, cabbage and a bowl of lettuce. What's worse, Rose even saw some lettuce were moving. Rosa looked a bit more closely and saw that the lettuce bowl was full of ants, hundreds of them. And then they told us that because of the hurricane, there were no flights to San Antonio, and that they had to stay there for another three days, three more days in that place... there was nothing to do, nowhere to go, they couldn't eat the food. It was noisy and dirty.

You know, when they finally arrived in San Antonio, they were five days late. And the worst thing was that Hurricane had never arrived there. The weather had been perfect in San Antonio all the time ...

❧ Notes ❧

1. holiday from hell　糟糕的假期
2. the Caribbean　加勒比海
3. brochure　*n.*　宣传册，宣传页
4. hurricane　*n.*　飓风

Part Ⅴ　Skill Training

Ⅰ. Matches.

a. awful
b. renowned
c. representative
d. proceed to
e. valuables
f. belongings
g. inconceivable
h. nuisance
i. remedy
j. recurrence

1. 补救
2. 麻烦事
3. 再次发生
4. 贵重物品
5. 前往
6. 不可思议的
7. 私有财产，个人物品
8. 有名的，享有盛誉的
9. 糟糕的
10. 负责人，代表

Ⅱ. Career skills.

Read the following tourists' complaints first and discuss with your partner to i-dentify what complaints are reasonable and need to be resolved，and who has to be responsible for them.

1. The outward flight was delayed at the airport due to the unexpected heavy snow. And there was no representative from the travel service to help deal with the situation.

2. The tour guide arrived 20 minutes late to pick us up on the second day and didn't give excuses.

3. The hotel was reasonably comfortable but the food lacked variety.

4. Shops in resort were crowded and expensive.

5. Although advertised as a stone thrown from the beach，the hotel is in fact 20-minute walk away.

6. The Grape Valley visit was taken from schedule.

7. The tour guide asked for tips privately.

8. The return flight was scheduled for 9：10 am which meant having to leave the resort at dawn to get to the airport on time. As a result，the stay is not seven days.

Ⅲ. Translate the following sentences into Chinese.

1. I think I ought to apologize，not you.

2. I know you didn't mean it.

3. Please accept my deep apologies.

4. I can't tell you how sorry I am.

5. Sorry to have kept you waiting.

6. Oh ，sorry to hear that.

7. I will look into the matter.

8. This is quite unusual.

9. I am terribly sorry，sir. We are short of hands.

10. That's all right. Don't think any more about it.

Ⅳ. Translate the following sentence into English.

1. 由于意外大雪航班延迟。有没有代表在旅游服务中帮助处理？

2. 为了提高市场竞争力，旅行社通常付给导游很低的报酬，这使得工资之外的小费与佣金几乎成为导游获取相对较好收入的唯一途径。

3. 这家酒店相当舒适，但食物品种较少。

4. 酒店在竞争中采取一些更加贴心的服务。

5. 游客的投诉一定要及时有效地处理。

Ⅴ. Situational play.

Situation 1

Diner：One of the dishes isn't what you ordered. You tell the waiter to check the order and change it right now.

Waiter：The diner complains to you. Apologize to him and promise to get the dish ready soon. After that，ask the diner if he'd like something else.

Situation 2

Guest：After checking in the hotel，you find your room is next to a busy main road. You go to the front office and ask them to get you a quiet room.

Clerk：Apologize to him and help him to check if there is another room available.

Situation 3

Tourist：You attended a package tour to Shanghai. You felt so angry with the local guide，because she added too much extra shopping activities and extended the shopping time without permission. Now you are complaining this with the tour operator.

Tour Operator：Apologize to him and promise to look into this matter.

Part Ⅵ　Knowledge Expansion

五个典型案例分析

案例一：行程安排不周，旅行社需承担违约责任

案例：刘某一家三口于 2012 年 4 月 30 日报名参加了某旅行社组织的北京 4 日游，付清了旅游费用，并签订了旅游合同。按照合同约定，应是第 1 天 18：30 准时出发。刘某一家三口按时到达出发地点，但该团直到 20：30 才出发。到达北京后，旅行社又没按合同约定组织看升国旗、赠天安门集体照、游清华北大外景和皇城根遗址公园；进入故宫后，导游未提供讲解服务；因所租用车辆手续不全被扣押导致比规定时间晚一天返程。刘某遂投诉该家旅行社，经旅游监管大队调解，由旅行社一次性赔偿刘某600 元违约金。

分析：国家旅游局发布的《旅游行业对客人服务的基本标准（试行）》中对旅行社服务基本标准有这样的规定，除人力不可抗拒的因素外，属于旅行社工作疏漏，致使旅游团减少服务项目或延误旅游时间，旅行社应退还未提供服务项目的费用，并给予一定的赔偿。未按规定时间出发，未组织看升国旗、拍集体照，游客晚返程一天均是因为旅行社安排行程、租用车辆不当造成的，所以旅行社应承担相应的违约责任。

提醒：面对旅行社违约，消费者不要忍气吞声，自认倒霉，合同约定即产生法律效力，任何一方违约都必须承担违约责任。

案例二：临时告知自费项目，旅行社被迫全额退款

案例：张女士到某旅行社报名参加境外旅游，工作人员向她推荐旅游线路、服务标准，张女士接受了。张女士交付旅游团费、旅行社出具旅游发票后，旅行社工作人员告知张女士，每一位游客在境外必须参加自费项目，办理护照的费用也由游客自己承担。张女士认为旅行社工作人员有意隐瞒事实真相，存在欺诈行为。

分析：经旅游管理部门协调，旅行社退还游客全额旅游团费，旅游行程被取消。

提醒：旅行社作为旅游服务的经营者，必须事先向游客履行告知、答复和解释义务，告知游客各种费用的支出。

案例三：旅游投诉有期限为 90 天

案例：李先生参加某旅行社组织的黄山游，第二晚入住山上某山庄，客人晚餐后要走 5 分钟的路程才能回到房间。当时天黑，李先生不慎扭伤了脚。客人返程后到医院治疗，经拍片发现脚踝关节骨折。李先生向旅行社提出赔偿。出团前，旅行社已为客人投保了旅游人身意外险，但因没有当地医院的医治报告，保险公司拒绝受理此案。李先生提出投诉，但已经超过投诉有效期了。最后，旅行社同意赔偿李先生医药费及相关费用，其他费用不予赔偿，但李先生不同意。

分析：根据《旅行社质量保证金赔偿暂行办法》的有关规定，该案例投诉时已超过受理期限（90 天）。考虑到游客的具体困难，旅游管理部门为双方进行协调达成协议，旅行社补偿医药费、护理费。

提醒：按照有关规定，旅游管理部门受理投诉的期限为 90 天，游客在旅游途中如遇服务质量问题应及时到旅游质监部门投诉。

案例四：取消旅游，游客需承担违约责任

案例：赵先生和某旅行社签订了赴某地旅游的合同。在出发前 1 天，赵先生突然生病，希望旅行社取消旅游行程，全额退还交纳的旅游团费。旅行社表示，机票已经购买，如果赵先生临时取消行程必须承担机票损失，并承担相应的违约责任。经测算，赵先生将损失 80％的旅游团费。

分析：由于旅行社购买的机票为团体机票，虽能获得较为优惠的折扣，但团体机票不得退票，也不得转签。所以，当旅行社购买了团体机票而游客又临时取消行程时，机票损失不可避免地产生。依据旅行社与赵先生在合同中约定的违约条款，旅行社可以向赵先生收取实际损失的费用和违约金。

提醒：在签订旅游合同后，双方当事人应当严格遵守约定，任何一方需要解除合同，都必须和对方协商并达成一致，否则就必须承担违约责任。

案例五：拒绝返程不可取，维权也应理性

案例：某旅行社组织了 30 人赴某地区旅游。按照合同约定，游客应当乘坐某次火车硬卧返程。地接社难以买到约定的车次车票，只购买到其他车次返程车票。游客明确表示无法接受，要求旅行社给予赔偿。由于双方分歧过大，结果游客拒绝返程，滞留在旅游目的地。

分析：组团社应当为游客提供约定车次火车票，而不能以其他车次火车票代替，旅行社应当承担由此给游客造成的损失。由于游客的滞留，人为地给旅行社和游客自身造成了不必要的损失。

提醒：游客应当理性维权。游客维权的途径有：与旅行社协商、向有关管理部门投诉、向仲裁机构提请仲裁、向人民法院提起民事诉讼。假如游客采用过激方式，就难以有效地维护自己的合法权益。

Chapter 10

Dealing with Emergencies

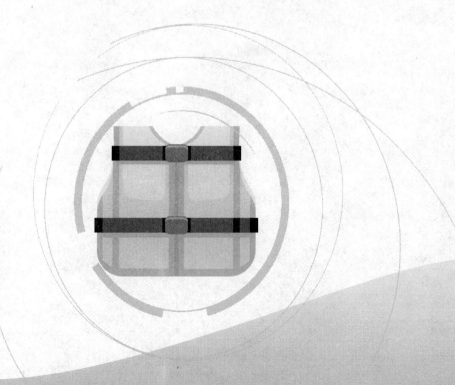

Part I Lead-in

【本章简介】

本章主要讲述旅游过程中，游客可能因为各种原因出现的一些紧急情况，如晕车、物品丢失、突发疾病等。本章通过情景对话和延伸阅读材料，讲解了导游在游客旅行过程中如果碰到这些情况应如何处理。

【教学目标】

1. 掌握与旅游紧急情况相关的专业英语词汇及用语；
2. 熟悉相应的处理过程，并且能够熟练地用英文表达；
3. 了解旅行中应提醒客人的注意事项；
4. 能够带领游客平安旅游。

【背景知识】

带团或者为游客服务时，导游应向游客介绍必要的安全常识和相关的防范措施。提醒游客不要擅自进入危险区域，提醒游客看管好所带财物，防止发生丢失、被盗现象；及时了解并向游客介绍所在饭店的安全通道，以备发生紧急情况时安全疏散游客。如遇到有可能危及游客人身安全的紧急情况，导游要灵活应变，在征求游客同意后，应及时调整行程，并立即报告旅行社。

Part II Situational Dialogues

Dialogue One

My Wallet Is Lost!

(At the souvenir shop.)

(T＝Tom，a tour guide   C＝Cindy)

T：What's the trouble with you?

C：My wallet is lost!

T：When did you notice that?

C：I kept it in my pocket. But just now when I wanted to buy a pack of chewing gum，I couldn't find it.

T：Where did you go after getting off the bus?

C：I just went to the grocery.

T：What's the color of your wallet and is there anything important in it?

C：It's black. There are two credit cards，some money and my passport in it.

T：Oh. Don't worry. You can go back to the grocery looking for it. If you can't find it，I will help you contact the police immediately.

C：Thank you!

Notes

1. lose   *v.* 丢失
2. pocket   *n.* 口袋
3. a pack of   一包
4. credit card   信用卡

Dialogue Two

You Look Pale

(A tourist party is sitting in the lobby of a hotel，waiting for their room keys.)

(A＝tourist   B＝tour guide)

A：Help! Help!

B：What's wrong with you? You look pale.

A：I feel dizzy and I have a terrible stomachache.

B：Have you ever had this kind of experience before?

A：No，I haven't.

B：What did you have for lunch?

A：I had two hamburgers，a beef steak，a vegetable salad and a huge ice cream.

B：Oh，you had a heavy meal.

A：What can I do now?

B：You can lie down on that sofa over there. I will call the Emergency Center at once.

Notes

1. pale *adj.* 苍白的

2. dizzy *adj.* 眩晕的；使人头晕的

3. a heavy meal 丰盛的食物

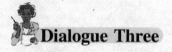

Dialogue Three

An Accident in a Restaurant

(A tourist has just broken a cup.)

(A＝tourist   B＝waiter)

A：Waiter，I'm sorry，I've broken this cup.

B：Never mind. I'll attend to it immediately. sir，you've injured your finger.

A：It's only a small cut.

B：Take it easy. I'll fetch a plaster for you.

(The waiter comes back in a while.)

B：Sir，let me help you.

A：Thank you very much.

B：You are most welcome.

Notes

1. attend to 照顾，照料

2. injure *v.* 伤害，受伤

3. a small cut 小伤口

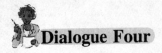

Dialogue Four

At Lost and Found Office

(Emma lost her digital camera and she went to the hotel's Lost and Found Office.)

(C=clerk   E=Emma)

C: What can I do for you, madam?

E: I can't find my digital camera.

C: When and where did you last use it?

E: I remember it was at the hotel lobby yesterday.

C: Could you give more details about the camera please?

E: It's a new silver Sony T700 camera. It's worth 2,500 yuan.

C: OK, madam. Please tell me your name and room number.

E: I'm Emma Brown. I'm staying at Room 1022.

C: (Write down the details in the Lost Property Report.) Thank you, madam. We'll try our best to look for your camera, and we'll contact you as soon as the camera is found.

Notes

1. digital camera　数码照相机
2. write down　写下
3. look for　寻找

Part Ⅲ　Vocabulary & Useful Expressions

Ⅰ. Useful Words

credit　*n.* 信用，信誉

passport   *n.* 护照

contact   *v.* 联系

experience   *n.* 经验

emergency   *n.* 紧急情况，突发事件

stomachache   *n.* 胃疼

accident   *n.* 事故，意外

attend   *v.* 照料，照顾

fetch   *v.* 取得，取来

plaster   *n.* 创可贴

finger   *n.* 手指

digital   *adj.* 数字的

camera   *n.* 照相机

lobby   *n.* （酒店的）大厅，休息室

detail   *n.* 细节，详情

silver   *adj.* 银的，银色的

worth   *n.* 价值   *adj.* 有价值的

property   *n.* 财物，财产

chewing gum   口香糖

beef steak   牛排

Emergency Centre   急救中心

Ⅱ. Useful Expressions

1. My wallet is lost!
   我的钱包丢了！

2. Where did you go after getting off the bus?
   您刚才下车后去哪儿了？

3. Is there anything important in your wallet?
   您的钱包里有什么贵重物品吗？

4. I will help you contact the police immediately.
   我马上帮您报警。

5. You look pale.
   您脸色苍白。

6. Have you ever had this kind of experience before?
   您以前有过类似的经历吗？

7. What did you have for supper?

   您晚饭吃的是什么?

8. You can lie down on that sofa over there.

   您可以躺在那边的沙发上。

9. I'll attend to it immediately.

   我会来收拾的。

10. Take it easy.

    别紧张。

11. I'll fetch a plaster for you.

    我去帮您拿个创可贴。

12. When and where did you last use it?

    您最后一次使用它是什么时间和什么地点?

13. Could you give more details about the camera please?

    您能告诉我数码相机的详细特征吗?

14. It's worth 2,500 yuan.

    价值 2 500 元。

Part Ⅳ　Reading Materials

Passage One

Dealing with Emergencies

The following emergencies happen quite often in service industries: loss, theft, fire, food poisoning, accident, complaint, etc. As a tour guide, it is important to deal with emergencies in a correct way because it will help to keep a good company image.

When you deal with emergencies, a quick response will satisfy customers. What is more, you need to look into the situation and listen to the customer's opinions carefully. Also, you need to try to solve problems in different ways for different situations. Do not forget that staying calm and taking quick and effective actions are the key to handling emergencies.

Notes

1. service industry   服务业
2. theft   *n.* 盗窃
3. deal with emergencies in a correct way   用正确的方式处理紧急事件
4. satisfy customers   使顾客满意
5. look into   调查
6. solve problems in different ways for different situations   针对不同的情况采取不同的解决方法
7. take actions   采取行动

 **Passage Two**

I work as a tour guide in a large tour agency. I often meet something interesting on the trip, but some emergency events also happen. For example, food poisoning sometimes may take place in a hotel. I would deal with the emergency in this way. First, I should keep calm and look into the situation. Then, I would call in a doctor and give some medicine to the customer. If the medicine does not help, I would send the customer to the hospital.

Notes

1. tour agency   旅行社
2. food poisoning   食物中毒
3. take place   发生
4. send...to...   送……到……

Part V Skill Training

Ⅰ. Matches.

a. accident	1. money available for a client to borrow
b. detail	2. having or causing a whirling sensation
c. attend	3. a document issued by a country to a citizen allowing that person to travel abroad
d. stomachache	4. an ache localized in the stomach or abdominal region
e. credit	5. the accumulation of knowledge or skill
f. dizzy	6. cause injuries or bodily harm to
g. lobby	7. take charge of or deal with
h. passport	8. a large entrance or reception room or area
i. experience	9. a small part that can be considered separately from the whole
j. injure	10. anything that happens by chance without an apparent cause

Ⅱ. Choices.

deal with	running	handling	emergencies	catching fire
details	satisfy	police	looking after	lying

1. What are the _____ that happen quite often in service industries?

2. Why is it important to _____ emergencies in a correct way?

3. What will _____ a customer?

4. What is the key to _____ emergencies?

5. A lady is ill in a hotel room. She is _____ in bed.

6. The elevator in the restaurant is not _____. People are pressing the emergency button.

7. A nurse is _____ a patient in an emergency room.

8. The hotel room is _____. They are running away.

9. A lady has lost a handbag, and she is looking for help at the _____.

10. Could you give me some _____ about your missing cellphone?

Ⅲ. Translate the following sentences into Chinese.

1. Where did you go after leaving the hotel?

2. You should probably inquire about your insurance policy regulations.

3. Please fill out these forms first.

4. I will attend to the accident.

5. I feel dizzy and I have a terrible stomachache.

Ⅳ. Translate the Chinese in brackets into English.

1. When you handle emergencies, the most important thing is to _____ (保持镇定).

2. _____ (食物中毒) is an emergency that sometimes takes place in hotels.

3. To _____ (解决问题), one must know clearly about the situation.

4. Being friendly and helpful will _____ (使顾客满意).

5. If you want to _____ a good _____ (保持形象), be honest with others.

Ⅴ. Situational play.

Situation 1

You are on a trip to South Korea. When you get off the plane, you cannot find your luggage.

Situation 2

Suppose you are a tour guide. One tourist had his leg broken when climbing a mountain. Please help to deal with the accident.

Part Ⅵ Knowledge Expansion

紧急情况的处理

外出旅游安全最重要，如果游客在旅途中遇到一些紧急情况，作为一名导游，该如何处理才能让游客有安全感呢？

1. 对晕动症的处理

晕车、晕船、晕机就是所谓的晕动症，其症状为打哈欠、脸色苍白、出汗等，严重的会出现头晕、恶心甚至呕吐等。晕动症以预防为主：导游应该告诉游客，在旅行

前放松心情，出行前保证睡眠充足；乘车前用餐不宜过饥也不宜过饱，不吃高蛋白、高脂肪类食品；还要提醒以前有晕动症的游客应尽量选择车厢内靠前且与行驶方向一致的座位，头部适当固定，眼睛自然注视前方，或提醒晕动症严重的游客在乘车前半小时或一小时服用晕动片。若有游客稍感不适，建议游客最好闭目养神或食用生姜片。

2. 对感冒的处理

游客旅行的目的地气候可能跟居住地差别较大，忽冷忽热，容易感冒。对于感冒首先要预防。旅行社应尽可能不组织游客到有可能发生流感的地方或疫区去；入住酒店时，导游应提醒游客保持室内空气流通；注意气候变化，提醒游客适时增减衣服。

3. 对肠胃病的处理

游客在旅游当中不适应新环境，不同地域的饮水和食物中所含元素不同，易引起腹胀和腹泻，如果再暴饮暴食，还易引起肠胃炎。因此，旅游途中导游要及时提醒游客注意饮食卫生，不吃不洁食物。尤其是内地游客初到海滨地区旅游，导游应告知游客吃海鲜的注意事项。如游客在旅途中不慎患上肠胃炎，需要及时送到当地医院进行治疗，尽量卧床休息，暂停进食 6～12 小时，多喝菜汤和淡盐水。

4. 对水土不服的处理

旅游时由于出门在外，气候、水质、饮食都与平日不同，一些人适应能力较差，会出现头昏、无力、食欲不振、难以入睡等水土不服的现象。如果旅行团中有游客出现这种情况，应建议游客多吃水果，少吃油腻食物，还可服用一些多酶片和维生素 B2。

5. 对中暑的处理

夏季炎热，如果游客长时间在户外活动，体内水分消耗过多，会导致中暑。中暑的人大多感觉头昏、耳鸣、恶心、无汗、眼睛发黑、呕吐和烦躁不安，严重的会导致昏迷。因此，旅行团夏季在户外活动时应尽量避开最炎热的中午，避免在烈日下长时间活动；提醒游客穿较为宽松、透气及吸汗性好的衣物并随温度的变化而增减衣物，太阳镜和太阳帽也是必不可少的遮阳装备；建议游客少量饮用茶水、淡盐水和补充含盐的食物。若游客已有中暑症状，应立即将其移到通风、凉爽的地方休息，并让其服用仁丹、十滴水，在太阳穴、人中处涂抹风油精。如病情较为严重应及时送往当地医院治疗。

6. 对咬伤的处理

在天气暖和的日子外出旅行难免会遭受昆虫叮咬，如果有游客被昆虫咬伤了，应建议其用碱性液体冲洗伤口，这样可以消除疼痛。如果游客被蛇咬伤了，首先必须查看伤口上的牙痕。如果有两个大牙痕，则是被毒蛇咬伤的，要立即用带子把伤口扎紧，防止毒素扩散。同时，要及时把毒素吸出或挤出，用肥皂水清洗伤口，然后尽快前往医院治疗。

Chapter 11

Chinese Local Activities

Part Ⅰ Lead-in

【本章简介】

本章主要讲述中国地方特色旅游活动的相关知识，如如何欣赏皮影戏、了解少数民族的一些风俗习惯以及宗教信仰等。读者通过情景对话和延伸阅读了解中国具有地方特色的一些旅游活动，最后通过练习进一步掌握旅游活动相关知识。

【教学目标】

1. 掌握中国地方特色旅游活动相关的英语专业词汇及用语；
2. 熟悉中国地方特色旅游活动的类型；
3. 了解中国地方特色旅游活动的文化和风俗；
4. 能够简要叙述中国地方特色旅游活动的基本概况。

【背景知识】

作为文明古国，中国具有悠久的历史和灿烂的文化，文化旅游资源十分丰富。这些文化旅游资源如民间传说、戏剧、宗教活动以及少数民族的传统节日等吸引着世界各地的游客。

Part Ⅱ Situational Dialogues

Dialogue One

Talking about Beijing Opera

(G＝guide   T＝tourist)

G：What do you feel after watching Beijing Opera? I do hope you enjoy it.

T：Well，I am a little amazed. It is quite different from our opera.

G：What do you think of the costumes?

T：It seems that they are very strange.

G：Yes，most of the costumes are in the Ming and Qing Dynasties' styles. How about the performance?

T：It is fantastic.

G：What is your opinion of the characters?

T：They are very impressive. The facial make-up helps a lot.

G：How do you feel about the music?

T：Absolutely stunning. Their voices are rather marvelous.

G：What do you think of the martial arts? Do you like it?

T：Great! I have never seen it before.

G：I am glad to hear that.

 Notes

1. Ming and Qing Dynasties　明清时期
2. fantastic　*adj.* 极好的，不可思议的
3. martial arts　武术

 **Dialogue Two**

Shadow Play

(A＝guide　　B＝foreign visitor)

A：Good evening. You look very excited after a whole day's sightseeing.

B：Yeah. I am looking forward to the recreational program in the evening.

A：Oh，I see. The program for this evening is Shadow Play.

B：Sounds great! Is it interesting?

A：Sure. It is one of the most ancient and famous Chinese folk performances.

B：Really? Would you mind telling me something about it?

A：The history of Shadow Play has a long history; it can be traced back to the Han Dynasty，more than 2,000 years ago.

B：Well，how about the performance?

A：Shadow Play performance is pretty interesting. Illuminated puppet figures are manipulated by three to five artists using a transparent white cloth screen now form an artistic combination of opera，music，fine art and special craftsmanship. Shadow Play combines the artistic elements of opera，music，fine arts and special craftsmanship.

B：Fantastic! Oriental arts have their special charms. I can't wait to see it!

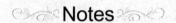

Notes

1. Han Dynasty   汉朝
2. illuminate   *v.* 照明，使照亮
3. manipulate   *v.* 操作，控制
4. oriental   *adj.* 东方的

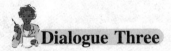 **Dialogue Three**

The Water Splashing Festival

（A＝foreign visitor   B＝guide）

A：Can you tell me something about the Water Splashing Festival?

B：Sure. The Water Splashing Festival is one of the Chinese minority festivals held by Dai Nationality. It is an expression of gratitude for the women for keeping the local people from being harmed.

A：Amazing!

B：It is said that there lived a demon king. He took seven women as his wives against their will. The women finally rose in rebellion and killed the demon king. However，the chopped head of the demon king kept rolling and caused fire. The fire could not be put out and thus the women took turns to hold the head once a year. When one woman's turn was over，the local people would splash water on her to rinse her of the blood and expel the evil spirits out of her.

A：Sounds moving! By the way，is the demon king dead finally?

B：Yes. With the passing of time，the demon king's head was finally burned to a-

shes. Splashing water on each other has gradually evolved into part of local customs.

A：I see. Are there any other activities along with the festival?

B：Yeah，such as dragon-boat racing，sending off skyrockets and throwing love pouches.

A：What does the throwing love pouches mean?

B：It is believed that the one thrown at by a girl is liked by her.

A：Pretty interesting.

B：It is said that everyone who is splashed at will have good luck.

A：Really? I can't wait to join in the activity.

B：I do hope you enjoy it.

Notes

1. Dai Nationality 傣族
2. gratitude *n.* 感谢，谢意
3. demon *n.* 魔鬼，恶魔
4. rebellion *n.* 反抗，抗议

Dialogue Four

Folk Paper-cut

(A＝guide   B＝foreign visitor)

A：Good morning，everyone. Today we will take part in the paper-cut activities.

B：Can you tell us something about it?

A：Sure. Paper-cutting is the product of folk customs of many nationalities in south China. It is popularly used as a decoration for festival gifts and sacrifices in the rural areas.

B：Will the local people teach us to do it?

A：Yes. They can teach us to make the window-flower，which is the major form of paper-cut.

B：Are there other forms of paper-cut?

A：Well，such as opera figures，birds and beasts，flowers and trees，and beautiful butterflies.

B：Does the paper-cut take us a long time to learn?

A：Maybe. Generally speaking，most paper-cut artists are women in the countryside and they are expected to learn it when they are young. But we can learn to do the simple one in a short time.

B：Great! I am looking forward to doing it.

Notes

1. decoration   *n.* 装饰
2. sacrifice   *n.* 祭祀
3. window-flower   *n.* 窗花
4. expect   *v.* 期望

Part Ⅲ   Vocabulary & Useful Expressions

mosque   *n.* 清真寺

handcraft   *n.* 手工，手艺

paper-cut   *n.* 剪纸

folklore   *n.* 民间传说

Shadow Play   皮影戏

puppet figures   木偶影子

facial make-up   脸谱

Water Splashing Festival   泼水节

Torch Festival   火把节

Tibetan New Year   藏历新年

dragon-boat racing   龙舟赛

sending off skyrockets   流星焰火

throwing love pouches   抛绣球

Part Ⅳ   Reading Materials

**Passage One**

History of Shadow Puppets

More than 2,000 years ago, a favorite concubine of Wu Emperor of the Han Dynasty died of illness, the emperor missed her so much that he lost his desire to reign. One day, a minister happened to see children playing with dolls where the shadows on the floor were vivid. Inspired by this scene, the smart minister hit upon an idea. He made a cotton puppet of the concubine and painted it. As night fell, he invited the emperor to watch a rear-illuminated puppet show behind a curtain. The emperor was delighted and took to it from then on. This story recorded in the official history book is believed to be the origin of shadow puppetry.

Shadow puppets were first made of paper sculpture, later from the hides of donkeys or oxen. That's why the Chinese name for shadow puppet is Pi Ying, which means shadows of hides. Shadow puppetry was very popular during the Tang and Song Dynasties in many parts of China.

Shadow puppetry was related to politics. In Beijing, for example, during the reign of Emperor Kangxi, this folk art was so popular that there were eight generously paid puppeteers in one prince's mansion. When the Manchu rulers spread their rule to various parts of China, they brought the puppet show with them to make up for the fact that they could not appreciate local entertainment due to language barriers. From 1796 to 1800, the government forbade the public showing of puppet shows to prevent the spreading of peasant uprising at the time. It was not until 1821 that shadow puppet shows gained some vigor.

Today, shadow puppet shows face extinction like other traditional art forms such as Nuo Drama.

Shadow puppetry wins the heart of an audience by its lingering music, exquisite sculpture, brisk color and lively performance.

One mouth tells stories of thousands of years; a pair of hands operates millions of soldiers. This is how the shadow puppeteer works. Nicknamed the business of the five, a shadow puppet troupe is made up of five people. One operates the puppets, one plays a horn, a suo-na horn, and a yu-kin, one plays banhu fiddle, one is in charge of percussion instruments, and one sings. This singer assumes all the roles in the puppet show, which of course is very difficult. That is not all, the singer also plays several of over 20 kinds of musical instruments in a puppet show. These ancient musical instruments enhance this ancient folk art.

The stage for shadow puppet is a white cloth screen on which the shadows of flat puppets are projected. Shadow puppet looks similar to paper-cut except that their joints are connected by thread so that they can be operated freely. The scene is simple and primitive; it is the consummate performance that attracts the audience. For example, a puppet can smoke and breathe out a smoke ring "C" with the operator's help. In one drama, as a maid sits in front of a mirror, her reflection matches her actions. The operator plays five puppets at the same time, each of which has three threads. Ten fingers handle 15 threads. No wonder the operator is compared to the 1,000-hand Kwan-yin （观音）.

To overcome the limit imposed when only the profile of puppets can be seen, shadow puppets use exaggeration and heavy dramatization. The faces and the costumes of puppets are vivid and humorous. The flowery color, the elegant sculpting and smooth lines make shadow puppets not only props but also artwork. A shadow puppet takes as many as 24 procedures and more than 3,000 cuts.

The figures all have a large head and a small body, which tapers down. A man has a big head and a square face, a broad forehead and a tall strong body without being too masculine. A woman has a thin face, a small mouth and a slim body without being too plump. Effeminacy and tenderness are the norm for Chinese beauty. Scholars wear long robes with an elegant demeanor while generals in martial attire bring to mind bravery and prowess.

The design of the figures follows traditional moral evaluation and aesthetics. The audience can tell a figure's character by seeing his mask. Like the masks in Beijing Opera, a red mask represents uprightness, a black mask, fidelity, and a white one, treachery. The positive figure has long narrow eyes, a small mouth and a straight bridge of nose, while the negative one has small eyes, a protruding forehead and sagging mouth. The clown has a circle around his eyes projecting a humorous and frivolous air even before he performs any act.

Lavish background pieces including architecture, furniture, vessels and auspicious patterns are featured in shadow puppet shows. Earthy art that it is, shadow puppet shows impress audiences by their vividness and refinement. A framed puppet can be a novel and pleasant souvenir.

Besides the figures needed in a certain drama, the shadow puppets include heroes from folklore and history, such as the four ancient beauties, Xi Shi, Wang Zhaojun, Diao Chan, and Yang Guifei; or the Monkey King, Emperor Qin Shihuang.

Shadow puppetry in Shaanxi is believed to be the most typical. The Ancient Cultural Street of Shuyuanmen is an ideal place to choose shadow puppets as souvenirs. Here you can select from hundreds of figures in different sizes and poses. Shadow puppets reveal a special world with their different figures.

Notes

1. reign   *n.* 统治
2. vivid   *adj.* 生动的，形象的
3. Manchu   *n.* 满族人，满语   *adj.* 满族的，满语的
4. barrier   *n.* 障碍
5. exquisite   *adj.* 精致的
6. musical instruments   乐器
7. exaggeration   *n.* 夸张
8. dramatization   *n.* 戏剧化
9. mask   *n.* 面具
10. souvenirs   *n.* 纪念品
11. reveal   *v.* 显示，揭示

 **Passage Two**

Paper-cut

Paper-cut is a very distinctive visual art of Chinese handicrafts. It originated from the 6th century when women used to paste golden and silver foil cuttings onto their hair at the temples, and men used them in sacred rituals. Later, they were used during festivals to decorate gates and windows. After hundreds of years' development, now they have become a very popular means of decoration among country folk, especially women.

The main cutting tools are simple: paper and scissors or an engraving knife, but clever and deft craftspeople are remarkably good at cutting in the theme of daily life. When you look at items made in this method carefully, you will be amazed by the true to life expressions of the figure's sentiment and appearance, or portrayal of natural plants and animals' diverse gestures.

Although other art forms, like painting, can also show similar scenes, paper cutting still stands out for its charm—exacting lines and ingenious patterns which are all hand-made. To make the three-dimensional scenes pop out visually from the paper, as they are usually in monochrome, engravers must exert their imagination. They must delete secondary parts and compose the main body properly, abstractly and boldly. Though simple, the color then appears charmingly bright.

It is easy to learn about cutting a piece of paper but very difficult to master it with perfection. One must grasp the knife in an upright fashion and press evenly on the paper with some strength. Flexibility is required but any hesitation or wiggling will lead to imprecision or damage the whole image. Engravers stress the cutting lines in several styles. They attempt to carve a circle like the moon, a straight line like a stem of wheat, a square like a brick, and a jagged line like a beard.

People find hope and comfort in expressing wishes with paper-cuttings. For example, for a wedding ceremony, red paper-cuttings are a traditional and required decoration on the tea set, the dressing table glass and on other furniture. A big red paper character "Xi" (happiness) is a traditional must on the newlywed's door. Upon the birthday party of a senior, the character "Shou" represents longevity and will add delight to the whole celebration; while a pattern of plump children cuddling fish signifies that every year they will be abundant in wealth.

Notes

1. distinctive *adj.* 有特色的，与众不同的
2. scissors *n.* 剪刀
3. wedding ceremony 婚礼仪式
4. longevity *n.* 长寿

5. abundant *adj.* 大量的，丰盛的

Part Ⅴ   Skill Training

Ⅰ. Matches.

a. demon   1. 民间传说
b. manipulate   2. 戏剧化
c. decoration   3. 皮影戏
d. folklore   4. 大量的，丰盛的
e. puppet figures   5. 泼水节
f. Shadow Play   6. 装饰
g. paper-cut   7. 魔鬼，恶魔
h. Water Splashing Festival   8. 木偶影子
i. abundant   9. 操作，控制
j. dramatization   10. 剪纸

Ⅱ. Choices.

folk	related	puppets	perfection	scissors	customs
minority	origin	craftsmanship	cuttings		

1. Shadow Play combines the artistic elements of opera, music, fine arts and special _____.

2. The Water Splashing Festival is one of the Chinese _____ festivals held by Dai Nationality.

3. Paper-cutting is the product of _____ customs of many nationalities in south China.

4. Shadow _____ were first made of paper sculpture, later from the hides of donkeys or oxen.

5. The main cutting tools are simple：paper and _____ or an engraving knife.

6. People find hope and comfort in expressing wishes with paper _____.

7. It is easy to learn about cutting a piece of paper but very difficult to master it

with _____.

8. Splashing water on each other has gradually evolved into part of local _____.

9. Shadow puppetry was _____ to politics.

10. This story recorded in the official history book is believed to be the _____ of shadow puppetry.

Ⅲ. Translate the following sentences into Chinese.

1. Shadow Play combines the artistic elements of opera, music, fine arts and special craftsmanship.

2. The Water Splashing Festival is one of the Chinese minority festivals held by Dai Nationality.

3. Paper-cutting is the product of folk customs of many nationalities in south China.

4. Shadow puppetry wins the heart of an audience by its lingering music, exquisite sculpture, brisk color and lively performance.

5. People find hope and comfort in expressing wishes with paper-cuttings.

Ⅳ. Translate the following expressions into English.
1. 皮影戏
2. 木偶影子
3. 龙舟赛
4. 抛绣球
5. 泼水节

Ⅴ. Oral practice.
1. Please name different kinds of Chinese local activities.
2. Please give a brief introduction about Beijing Opera.

Part Ⅵ　Knowledge Expansion

藏历新年

藏历新年是藏族人民一年中最为隆重的传统节日，从藏历元月一日开始，到十五

日结束，持续十五天。因为藏族人民信仰佛教，节日活动洋溢着浓厚的宗教气氛，是一个娱神和娱人、庆祝和祈祷兼具的民族节日。

准备"切玛"

藏历新年的准备工作一般在前一年的十二月初就开始了。除购置吃喝玩乐的年货外，家家户户都要制作一个名叫"切玛"的五谷斗，即在绘有彩色花纹的木盒左右分别盛放炒麦粒和酥油拌成的糌粑，上面插上青稞穗和酥油塑制的彩花。还要用水浸泡一碗青稞种子，使其在新年时节长出一两寸长的青苗。"切玛"和麦苗供奉在神案正中，祈祷来年五谷丰登。

制作"卡赛"

临近节日，男人们忙着打扫庭院，女人们则精心制作"卡赛"——一种酥油炸成的面食，分为耳朵形、蝴蝶形、条形、方形、圆形等各种形状，涂以颜料，裹以砂糖。"卡赛"既是装饰神案的艺术品，又是款待客人的佳肴。"卡赛"的品种花色常常成为女主人勤劳、智慧和热情的象征，在节日里格外引人注目。

"古突"习俗

十二月二十九日进入除夕。这天，要给窗户门换上新布帘，在房顶插上簇新的经幡，门前、房梁和厨房也要用白粉画上吉祥图案，营造喜庆的气氛。入夜，全家老少围坐在一起吃一顿例行的"古突"。"古突"是用面疙瘩、羊肉、人参果煮成的饭。家庭主妇在煮饭前悄悄在一些面疙瘩里分别包进石头、羊毛、辣椒、木炭、硬币等物品。吃到这些东西的人必须当众吐出来，预兆此人的命运和心地。石头代表心狠，羊毛代表心软，木炭代表心黑，辣椒代表嘴巴不饶人，硬币预示财运亨通。

大年三十晚上，家庭主妇要准备团圆饭，与汉族的年夜饭相似。晚餐前，如家有僧人，由他先在经堂里诵祝愿经或称祈祷经，经备在经堂神龛上，平放堆满青稞、酥油，并插上象征吉祥的八宝图木板，还要点燃酥油灯和藏香。饭后一般边喝酥油茶、青稞酒边聊天。

大年初一这天，家庭主妇起得最早。五点钟左右就要煮一锅"羌枯"，即放有糌粑、红糖和奶渣的青稞酒，给每人送上一碗。家人尚未起床，就在被窝里喝碗"羌枯"，继续蒙头睡觉。主妇则坐在窗前等待日出，当东方晨曦初露，便匆匆背上水桶去河边或水井汲取新年的第一桶水。传说这时的水最为圣洁、清甜，最先打上吉祥水的家庭，在新的一年里就能免去许多灾难。天亮了，全家人都穿上新衣服，洗漱完毕，晚辈就开始向长辈恭贺新年，互道"扎西德勒"（吉祥如意）；然后开始吃早餐，互敬青稞酒。在牧区，主妇按照家庭成员的数目煮好羊头，用食案捧到年龄最长的男子面前，由他依长幼的次序分发给每人一只羊头、一把小刀。大家围着火炉一面剥羊头肉吃，一面互祝新年家庭和睦，人增畜旺。大年初一这天，一般都闭门谢客。大街上很冷清，人们都在家里举行庆祝和佛事活动。

亲朋好友从初二开始串门拜年。客人登门必道"洛萨扎西德勒（新年好）"，主人捧起"切玛"到门口迎接客人，客人先用拇指、食指和中指拈起一撮糌粑、几粒青稞抛向天空，表示敬神，再拈起一撮糌粑和青稞送进自己嘴里，感谢主人的盛情，然后入座饮酒聊天。从这天起，民间艺人也四处活动，演唱藏戏和"折嘎"（藏族曲种。"折嘎"意为吉祥的果实。演唱"折嘎"有送吉祥、传好运的意思）。

富裕的人家提前与民间艺人约好，准时来家里演唱，与客人共享。没有得到邀请的艺人也可主动上门演唱。"折嘎"艺人头戴白面具，手持木棍，用即兴编唱的歌词愉悦主人，如女主人多么美丽，男主人多么睿智，新年里一定会走好运等，一般都能得到好酒好肉的酬劳。在街头和村子里，人们还举行群众性的歌舞和藏戏演出活动。这种相互拜访和自娱性的文艺活动要持续三至五天，然后逐步转入以娱神为主的佛事活动。在拉萨地区主要是参加传昭法会，在东部昌都和北部羌塘草原，人们开始转山朝佛，给寺庙布施上香，祈祷新年风调雨顺、国泰民安。

藏历正月初三敬奉"屋脊神"，这天，人们都登上各家的屋顶，把崭新的经幡插在屋顶上，然后煨燃柏枝，向空中抛洒糌粑，飘动的经幡和袅袅上升的"桑烟"寄托着人们的祈愿。

从初三或初四起，举行西藏最大的宗教节日——传昭大法会（又称为莫朗钦波节）。这一法会是由格鲁派创始人宗喀巴于 1409 年在拉萨发起的一次祈愿大法会延续而来的。法会期间，西藏三大寺的僧人集中在大昭寺向释迦牟尼的佛像祈祷，并举行格西学位的考试。除政府给僧众发放布施外，西藏及其他地方的藏传佛教信众也到此添灯供佛、放布施。

藏历正月初五，拉萨郊区的农民要举行隆重的开犁礼。人们穿上节日的盛装，耕牛的额头上贴着酥油图案，犄角上插着彩旗和彩色羽毛，牛轭上披挂着缀满贝壳和松石的彩缎，尾巴上系着五彩缤纷的绸带，俨然一副"花枝招展"的模样。开耕之前，要从家里扛出一块白色山石，那是前一年从农田请回收藏好的，重新恭恭敬敬地安入农田中央，称为"阿妈色多"，意即"金石头妈妈"，是庄稼的保护女神。人们在地里煨起桑烟，插上祈福幡，赶着牛，围绕白石耕出五条畦子。每一畦撒播一种作物，例如豌豆、青稞、小麦、油菜子、蚕豆等。开犁礼完毕，大家会聚一处，一边喝酒一边唱歌，随着酒碗的轮转，歌声弥漫在整个初春的河谷，直到太阳西沉，尽兴而归。

Chapter 12

Red Tourism

Part I   Lead-in

【本章简介】

本章主要讲述旅游发展新趋势中的一种重要旅游形式——红色旅游。红色旅游主要表现为了解中国红色革命景点的人文历史与宣扬革命情怀。读者通过情景对话以及延伸阅读等了解红色旅游在中国的发展及前景，最后通过练习进一步掌握红色旅游方面的知识。

【教学目标】

1. 掌握与红色旅游相关的英语专业词汇及用语；
2. 熟悉红色旅游的流程，并能用英语熟练地表达；
3. 了解中国红色旅游的特点及景点；
4. 能够以恰当的方式引导游客进行红色旅游。

【背景知识】

红色旅游作为一种新型的主题旅游形式，日益受到国内外游客的重视和青睐。游客不仅可以观光赏景，而且更重要的是可以了解革命历史，学习革命斗争精神，培养新时代奋斗精神。作为一名导游，应尽可能详尽地了解红色景点的历史背景，注意将红色旅游的学习性、娱乐性与参与性结合起来，力求红色旅游活动"原汁原味、有惊无险、苦中有乐、先苦后甜"，最大限度地满足游客的精神诉求。

Part II   Situational Dialogues

Dialogue One

(At the travel agency.)

(A＝tour guide   B＝tour leader)

A：Good morning, Mr. Benjamin. I'd like to talk about the itinerary for your trip. Can you spare me some time?

B：Sure. We received a copy of the itinerary from your travel agency. I hope there haven't been any changes.

A：No change at all. Everything will be followed right as we have made.

B：That's all right.

A：First there will be a one-day visit in Nanchang. Then we will leave for Jinggangshan by bus.

B：How long will the trip take by bus?

A：2 hours. I'm sure we'll have an unforgettable experience during our stay at Jinggangshan.

B：Great, I'm eager to enjoy it as early as possible.

A：Moreover, we'll stay in Jiujiang for 2 days. After that, we leave Jiujiang for home by air. The whole trip will last 6 days. Wish all of you health in this long journey.

B：No problem.

A：Good. If there should be any changes, please let me know in advance.

B：Sure. Thank you for all you've done for us.

Notes

1. Can you spare me some time?　您能抽出点时间给我吗？
2. a copy of the itinerary　行程的复印件
3. in advance　提前

Dialogue Two

(On the way to the scenic spot.)

(A＝tour guide　　B＝tourist)

A：How lucky we have such a fine day today to go to the Hongyan Revolutionary Memorial Museum. It is located at Yuzhong District. And we will get there in ten minutes by car.

B：By the way, could you briefly give us some information about it? We really want to know something about it.

A: Certainly, sir. The Hongyan Revolutionary Memorial Museum used to be the base of the Southern Bureau of the CPC Central Committee and the Chongqing office of the Eight Route Army during the period of Anti-Japanese War. It opened as a memorial museum on May 1st, 1958, and is now considered one of China's most important monuments.

B: Oh, we're looking forward to seeing it.

A: Besides the museum building, the Hongyan Revolutionary Memorial Museum also includes several famous revolutionary and historical sites, such as the Zhou Residence (where Zhou Enlai had lived and worked as the chief representative of the CPC in Chongqing Negotiation), and the Gui Garden (where the October 10th Agreement was signed between the CPC and Nationalist Party, marking temporary peace between the two parties).

B: Sounds great.

A: Yes, it's a very precious and priceless treasure in China. Many people are willing to get more understanding about Hongyan spirit.

B: Thank you for your explanation.

A: My pleasure.

Notes

1. Hongyan Revolutionary Memorial Museum   红岩革命纪念馆
2. briefly *adv.* 简明扼要地
3. CPC: Communist Party of China   中国共产党
4. sign the agreement   签署协议

Dialogue Three

(Laura and George meet with a Chinese festival and plan to go to the Former Residence of Mao Zedong.)

(G=George   L=Laura   T=tour guide)

G: So many people here! What's that? It seems to be an interesting game.

T：We are lucky today. It's the Kite Festival in China.

L：Oh, flying kites! I've heard of it before, but this is the first time I have seen the real one.

G：We can go there and buy one to fly. Wanna try?

L：Maybe next time. I'd prefer watching others fly them now. Look, the old man's kite is a dragon. It's so fantastic in the sky.

T：Now, we'll move to visit the next destination, which is related to the greatest leader Chairman Mao. Yeah, it is the Former Residence of Mao Zedong.

G：Pretty good. I can't wait to see his residence!

L：Could you tell us something about him?

T：Yes, he was the leader of China's revolution. And with his leadership, the Chinese people founded the new People's Republic of China. Moreover, he is a talented poet, calligrapher and writer. His political writings are influential in the development of Marxist thought and his poetry retains some popularity in China now.

G：Very cool. I have learned several of his poems. They are really good stuff.

L：I know he stood on the Tian'anmen Rostrum in 1949, announcing the foundation of People's Republic of China.

T：Right. I'm sure you will be more interested in his former surroundings and get more details about his lifetime stories and achievements.

Notes

1. the Former Residence of Mao Zedong   毛泽东故居
2. They are really good stuff.   它们确实不错。
3. Tian'anmen Rostrum   天安门城楼

Dialogue Four

（A tour guide and his American tourist are at the scenic spot of the Memorial Garden of the Red Woman Detachment now.)

（A＝tour guide　　B＝tourist）

A：Now，we are at the Memorial Garden of the Red Woman Detachment.

B：It's really a big garden，isn't it?

A：Yes，it is. This memorial garden covers an area of 200 mu，and has six main parts，that is，the Museum of Red Woman Detachment，the Former Residence of Local Tyrant Nan Batian，Dancing and singing Square，Peace Square，Memorial Square，Coconut Forest Village.

B：What a grand garden！

A：Yes. You can get better understanding of the revolutionary history of Red Woman Detachment.

B：Could you tell me something about the Red Woman Detachment?

A：OK. It was founded in Neiyuan Village，Lehui County，Hainan Province on May 1st，1931. It is the first revolutionary armed force organized by women in the modern history of China.

B：I have heard that they were brave and they fought the enemies bravely on the battlefield.

A．Yes，the Red Woman Detachment made a good military exploit and they were well-known in Hainan.

（Having finished visiting the first five parts of the memorial garden. ）

A：Now，let's taste the fresh and delicious coconut juice in the Coconut Forest Village，where you may relax yourself and feel good in body and mind.

B：Pretty well. I love this place.

A：Well，our next scenic spot is the Wanquan River. It is the third longest river in Hainan Province.

B：Good. When shall we set out for it?

A：It is about 3 o'clock in the afternoon after we have the meal together.

B：OK.

Notes

1. Memorial Garden of the Red Woman Detachment　红色娘子军纪念园

2. Coconut Forest Village　椰子林

3. feel good in body and mind　感到身心愉悦

Part Ⅲ　Vocabulary & Useful Expressions

Ⅰ. Useful Words

patriotism　*n.* 爱国主义，爱国心

revolutionary　*adj.* 革命的

victory　*n.* 胜利

exhibit　*n.* 展品

contribute　*v.* 贡献；捐献

ethos　*n.* 民族精神；风气

achievement　*n.* 成就

launch　*v.* 发起；发动；开展

socialism　*n.* 社会主义

impressive　*adj.* 印象深刻的；令人佩服的

boom　*v.* 繁荣

relics　*n.* 遗迹

heroic　*adj.* 英雄的；英勇的

profound　*adj.* 意义深远的

guerilla　*n.* 游击队

exploit　*n.* 开拓；功绩

sacred　*adj.* 神圣的

wonder　*n.* 奇迹

headquarter　*n.* 总部，中心

liberate　*v.* 解放

memorial　*n.* 纪念馆；纪念碑；纪念物

hard-earned　*adj.* 来之不易的

military　*adj.* 军事的　*n.* 军队，军人

force　*n.* 力量；军队

battlefield　*n.* 战场

Left Adventurism　"左倾"冒险主义

Long March　长征

Nationalist Party　国民党

Ⅱ. Useful Expressions

1. What is this area famous for?

   此地以什么著名?

2. Could you recommend me some good places for this area?

   你能为我推荐一些这个地方的有名景点吗?

3. Can you recommend a sightseeing route for us?

   你可以帮助我们介绍一下旅游路线吗?

4. Sure, we have all kinds of routes. What kinds of places would you like to visit?

   没问题,我们有各种旅游路线。你们想到哪些地方玩?

5. I hope to get the detailed information about you so as to work out a good itinerary for you.

   我希望得到您的详细资料以便为您安排一个适合您的行程。

6. We provides all kinds of tours, such as individual tour, group package tour, specialized tours including red resorts tour, rural tour, regional tour, etc.

   我们提供各种旅游项目,如散客旅游、包团旅游,以及红色胜地旅游、乡村旅游、区域旅游等特色旅游。

7. Since this is the peak season in Shaoshan, you'd better make the reservation for it now.

   因为现在是韶山旅游的高峰期,您最好现在就预订好。

8. Would you take a picture of us all? All you have to do is to focus it.

   您能为我们拍张照片吗?您只需要把焦距对准就行了。

9. I'm sorry that photos are not allowed here.

   很抱歉,此处禁止拍照。

10. Now please come this way, and watch your step.

    请走这边,小心脚下,注意安全。

11. Thirty minutes later, we'll leave for the next scenic spot.

    半个小时后,我们将到下个景点进行游览。

12. Slow down please, I couldn't follow you.

    请慢点,我都跟不上你了。

13. Please keep an eye on the kids because it's so big and crowded.

    由于这里人多、地方大,请留心您的孩子。

14. Well, this is a must for many visitors.

    这里是许多游客的必到之处。

Part Ⅳ　Reading Materials

Passage One

Red Tourism

Red tourism is a new tourism product combination of patriotic education and the tourism industry. It means an activity to attract the tourists not only for visiting the revolutionary places and monuments, but also for aiming to get better understanding of the revolutionary spirits, to accept the revolutionary traditional education, to revivify, to relax and to widen the vision. Red tourism is a new style of theme tourism to integrate "Red Cultural Relics" with "Green Natural Sights", and to combine "Revolutionary Traditional Education" with "Promotion of Tourism Development". The tour routes and eternal scenic spots can provide the tourists the opportunities not only to enjoy the beautiful scenery, but also to understand the revolutionary history of China, to enrich the revolutionary knowledge, to learn the revolutionary struggle spirit, to foster the new era spirit and to make this tour become a kind of culture.

Red tourism is also popularly called "Revolutionary Sacred Places Tourism", which covers the old liberated areas, the revolutionary bases, and the great-man former residences and so on. These sacred places show us not only the simple revolutionary theme but also bring us to those unforgettable years of the gunfire licking the heavens, the fiery ages of the blood and war, those martyrs of shedding their blood and laying down their life, those dauntless historical great men, those historical moment bringing about a radical change in the situation. Furthermore, the old party members and old red armies revisit the old haunts, and they are lost in the myriad of thoughts; and the young people track down the red footmark, recall the revolutionary martyrs and get to know nowadays peace that is hard earned.

From Jinggangshan (Jinggang Mountain) to Ruijin, from Wayaobao to Yan'an, the Chinese Communist Party had always been at the head of the epoch, and had led the people to spend the unforgettable era. In 1927, Mao Zedong, Zhu De and other communists, led the Chinese Workers' and Peasants' Red Army establish the first rural revolutionary base in Jinggangshan. In the early of 1937, the Central Committee of the Communists Party of China garrisoned Yan'an. And the Stupa or Tope in Tang dynasty standing on the hill has become a treasury pagoda well-known far and near, besides, the Stupa has already become the great symbol of the democracy and revolution of China.

Shaoshan in Hunan Province is the hometown of Mao Zedong, the great man of an era. In the former residence of the great chief, in Nanan School, in the Peasant Evening School, and in the old address of the Peasant Activity in Xiangtan, the tourists can get the first-hand understanding of the traces of the great man; Nanchang in Jiangxi Province is a heroic city. Here the Chinese Communist Party began the first shooting to independently lead the revolutionary war; Zunyi in Guizhou Province, is a place of strategic importance in dynasties, where the Chinese Workers' and Peasants' Red Army withdrew the prologue to the Battle of Zunyi, and Tsunyi Meeting (Zunyi Conference) has become the important milestone in the revolutionary history of China.

Red tourism will make people, especially the young people, further deepen their belief in pursuing the road of socialism with Chinese characteristics and realizing the great rejuvenation of the nation under the leadership of the Communist Party of China. The great national spirits that grew out of the fights to win national independence are valuable in the revolutionary war periods and present-day efforts to realize the rejuvenation of the country.

Notes

1. patriotic *adj.* 爱国的
2. monument *n.* 纪念碑
3. revivify *v.* 使恢复活力；重新振兴
4. integrate *v.* 使完整；使合并
5. foster *v.* 培养；养育
6. fiery *adj.* 热烈的；炽热的；燃烧般的
7. martyr *n.* 烈士；殉道者
8. dauntless *adj.* 勇敢的；不屈不挠的
9. myriad *n.* 无数，极大数量
10. epoch *n.* 新纪元；新时代
11. the Central Committee of the Communists Party of China 中共中央

12. stupa　*n.* 佛塔

13. pagoda　*n.*（东方寺院的）宝塔

14. trace　*n.* 痕迹；踪迹

15. withdraw　*v.* 撤退；收回；拉开

16. prologue　*n.* 开场白；序言

17. milestone　*n.* 里程碑，划时代的事件

18. rejuvenation　*n.* 复壮；恢复活力；复原

 **Passage Two**

China to Further Expand Red Tourism

The year of 2011 is the 90th anniversary of the founding of the Communist Party of China, and red tourism is experiencing an unprecedented boom period. Many people want to "feel" China's history and raise their level of knowledge by visiting revolutionary sites. Red tourism is a subset of tourism in China in which Chinese people visit revolutionary sites with historical significance.

A national red tourism work meeting was held in Beijing on June 15, where the successful experiences of flourishing red tourism sites were summed up and the work for red tourism development in the next five years was also fully deployed. Liu Yunshan, member of the Political Bureau of CPC Central Committee, Secretary of the Secretariat of the CPC Central Committee and Minister of the Publicity Department of the CPC Central Committee, attended the meeting.

Red Tourism Sites Received Nearly 1. 4 Billion Tourists in the Past Six Years

Since the first-phase project was implemented six years ago, red tourism in China has received nearly 1. 4 billion tourists in total, according to Zhu Zhixin, director of the National Red Tourism Coordination Group.

In 2010, red tourism received 430 million tourists in total, accounting for 20 percent of all domestic tourists of the same year. In the same year, red tourism also created 912,000 direct jobs and more than 3. 7 million indirect jobs. Though several museums, memorials and patriotic education sites were free of charge, the total income from red tourism in 2010 still reached 130. 2 billion yuan. Red tourism has become an important part and a pillar of China's tourism business and brought in good political, social and economic benefits.

Under great support from the country, the old revolutionary base areas have completed 127 red tourism highway projects with a total length of 3,418 kilometers, successively accomplished the construction or reconstruction projects of many key red tourism airports including the Baise Airport, Jinggangshan Mountain Airport and Huai'an Airport, and built 106 railway stations in the past six years.

In the past six years, China also allocated 8 billion yuan of red tourism special construction funds in total. Local areas made remarkable progress in revolutionary historic cultural heritage protection, construction of infrastructural facilities of scenic sites and other aspects. Their exhibition levels, revolutionary site protection abilities, service levels and receiving capacities have all been improved significantly.

Red Cultural Products—A Feast for the Eyes

The enthusiasm of people participating in the red tourism has grown since the implementation of the first stage of planning. The source of tourists for red tourism scenic spots has gradually transformed from group tourism to both group tourism and individual tourism. Meanwhile, the reputation of red tourism scenic spots and of visitors' sense of identity is also rising.

The development of red tourism has given red culture popular support. Red tourism scenic spots in various places has further explored the cultural connotation and created popular red cultural products that reflect the core values of socialism. Red tourism scenic spots such as Xibaipo, Jinggangshan, Yan'an, Longyan, Linyi and Zunyi also established red stages to perform red shows for visitors. Performances such as "Jinggangshan" and "Dreaming Yan'an Defense Battle" are well received by visitors with their strong interaction.

Meanwhile, the development of red tourism also brought about a huge population flow, logistics flow, information flow and capital flow to the old revolutionary base areas. Locals actively participated in the development of red tourism and developed red tourism commodities and services to effectively expand employment, to increase their incomes and to promote the harmonious development of the economy and society in old revolutionary base areas.

Paying Attention to Historical and Cultural Heritage

The second phase of the plan to enrich red tourism content still focuses on the content related to China's revolutionary and wartime period, uses patriotism and traditional revolutionary spirits revealed in China since 1840 as themes and includes historical

and cultural heritage of representative events and figures into the scope of red tourism.

Hu Chengjun，deputy head of the office of the National Red Tourism Coordination Group，said the significance of expanding red tourism content lies in that it will benefit the inheritance of advanced culture and outstanding traditional spirit of the Chinese nation，help to make red tourism more consistent with the times and reality，further explore valuable spiritual wealth of red tourism and enrich the essence of red tourism.

The second phase of the plan includes targets for the development of red tourism over the next five years. Red tourism around the country will grow considerably during the 12th Five-Year Plan period.

It is expected that the number of visitors related to red tourism will exceed 800 million in 2015，representing an average annual growth rate of 15 percent and accounting for a quarter of the country's total. The comprehensive revenue of the red tourism sector will top 200 billion yuan，an average annual growth rate of 10 percent. The sector will directly create 500,000 new job opportunities and indirectly create 2 million new job opportunities.

Notes

1. Red tourism is experiencing an unprecedented boom period. 红色旅游正处于前所未有的大发展时期。

2. Red tourism has become an important part and a pillar of China's tourism business and brought in good political，social and economic benefits. 红色旅游已经成为中国旅游业的支柱，带来了良好的经济、政治和社会效益。

3. Their exhibition levels, revolutionary site protection abilities, service levels and receiving capacities have all been improved significantly. 这些红色旅游地区的展览能力、革命遗址保护能力、服务水平以及接待能力都得到了显著的提高。

4. Meanwhile，the development of red tourism also brought about a huge population flow, logistics flow, information flow and capital flow to the old revolutionary base areas. 同时，红色旅游将带动巨大的人员流、物资流、信息流以及资金流向老革命根据地倾斜。

5. It is expected that the number of visitors related to red tourism will exceed 800 million in 2015，representing an average annual growth rate of 15 percent and accounting for a quarter of the country's total. 据估计，到 2015 年有红色旅游

的游客总数将超过 8 亿人次，每年增幅将达到 15%，约占全国旅游总数的四分之一。

Part Ⅴ Skill Training

Ⅰ. Matches.

a. revolutionary bases

b. patriotic spirits

c. glorious tradition

d. backward economic conditions

e. Anti-Japanese War

f. proletarian revolutionist

g. spiritual prop

h. economic effect

i. liberation zone

j. refined route

1. 抗日战争

2. 精品路线

3. 红色根据地

4. 经济效益

5. 爱国精神

6. 解放区

7. 光荣传统

8. 落后的经济状况

9. 精神支柱

10. 无产阶级革命家

Ⅱ. Choices.

boom	charge	pillar	accounting	related
received	patriotic	benefits	also	though

Red tourism is a special tourism combining ___1___ education and the tourism industry, which is experiencing an unprecedented ___2___ period in China nowadays. In 2010, red tourism ___3___ 430 million tourists in total, ___4___ for 20 percent of all domestic tourists of the same year. In the same year, red tourism ___5___ created 912,000 direct jobs and more than 3.7 million indirect jobs. ___6___ several museums, memorials and patriotic education sites were free of ___7___, the total income from red tourism in 2010 still reached 130.2 billion yuan. Red tourism has become an important part and a ___8___ of China's tourism business and brought in good political, social and economic ___9___. It is expected that the number of visitors ___10___ to red tourism will exceed 800 million in 2015.

Ⅲ. **Translate the following sentences into Chinese.**

1. It is important to develop the red tourism in China and to launch widely the education of patriotism and revolutionary tradition.

2. Red tourism will provide more working opportunities and income for the local residents.

3. The revolutionary relics together with other tourism resources will be well developed and preserved.

4. As a revolutionary site as well as Chairman Mao Zedong's hometown, Shaoshan has caught a fever of red tourism.

5. Today, when tourists visit Jinggang Mountain, they can experience the hard life that Red Army soldiers endured: wearing coarse clothes, eating brown rice and pumpkin soup, and trekking along mountainous paths during the learning of their stories.

Ⅳ. **Translate the following sentences into English.**

1. 在抗日战争期间，一些著名的中国革命家如毛泽东、周恩来都曾经在此工作和生活过。

2. 红色旅游一般也称为革命圣地旅游，包括革命老区、革命根据地以及伟人故居等。

3. 大部分展品都在该建筑的一楼和二楼展出，都是一些陈旧的物品，包括旧家具、武器、有关起义的历史图片，但遗憾的是都是用中文介绍的。

4. 宝塔山也被称为"嘉岭山"，据说山上的宝塔始建于唐代，距今已经有 1 300 年的历史。

5. 韶山是一个距离长沙约 100 公里的山村，不仅有美丽的自然风景，具有典型的湖南乡村气息，而且有一段历史永远无法磨灭的革命战斗历程。

Ⅴ. **Situational play.**

Situation 1

You are a tourist guide, you are trying to arrange a trip for visiting Yan'an for two days. You may ask the tourists' needs and requests and make a good plan to reach their satisfaction.

(1) Ask the tourists' needs and requests for traveling Yan'an.

(2) Tell them your general plan for visiting Yan'an.

(3) Make some change according to their feedback.

(4) Make the final plan.

Situation 2

Suppose you are taking a group of British tourists to visit the Red Flag Canal in Linzhou, Henan Province. Most of the tourists want to enjoy the Red Flag Canal spirits on their own when traveling there.

(1) Guide them to watch the Red Flag Canal.

(2) Explain the background information for building it.

(3) Show some pictures and things about building it.

(4) Plan some specialty products for them to further their understanding of the Red Flag Canal.

Part VI   Knowledge Expansion

要成为一名优秀的导游，在引导游客游览过程中一定要把握适度的游览节奏 (sightseeing tempo)。要根据游览的内容调整节奏，不同的景点要安排好游览的不同时间。同时，导游需要注意不同的游客对游览节奏的快慢会有不同的需求，要充分考虑到游客们在年龄、身体状况及审美标准等方面的差异。在游览过程中，导游要设身处地地为游客考虑到景点的最佳观光时间及角度，使游客能够在有限的时间内尽可能体会到景点的独特之处。导游在沿途景点介绍过程中要做到有张有弛、动静结合，保证游览节奏有一定的变化，即可以在某些景点集中给游客讲解其中的历史典故、人文知识等，而在重要景点可以让游客有一定的时间自由游览和欣赏。适度的游览节奏不仅能够有助于游客感受丰富多彩的旅游景观，而且能够调节游客的体能，避免疲劳和各种事故，从而保证游览质量。

面对不同的游客群体，导游一定要有针对性地提供不同的导游服务。一般而言，游客旅游的目的包括观光、购物、度假、探险等，因此导游在为游客设计旅游行程时要充分考虑到他们旅游的目的，这样才能使游客保持良好的心情并配合导游完成整个

行程。当然，导游要根据游客的国籍（nationality）、职业（occupation）、年龄（age）、性别（sex）及社会地位（social status）等因素来确定他们的需求及预期。

　　总体来说，东方人比较内向，在表达观点或需求时通常较为含蓄；西方人比较直接，在表达观点或需求时通常开门见山。受过良好教育的游客会期望得到较为专业的导游服务，在景点的介绍方面需要更为全面而细致的讲解；一般游客则更偏爱简单的景点介绍，适时地多插入一些娱乐活动会受到他们的欢迎。年长的游客更注重旅游的安全性；年轻游客则更喜欢冒险，好奇心更强。女性游客一般喜欢购物，乐于接受故事性的景点讲解；男性游客则偏爱探险性、运动性的景点游览体验。

国内著名景点中英文对照

北京故宫（紫禁城）	The Imperial Palace（The Forbidden City）
长城	The Great Wall
颐和园	The Summer Palace
香山	The Fragrant Hill
天坛	The Temple of Heaven
天安门广场	Tian'anmen Square
亚运村	Asian Games Village
圆明园	Garden of Gardens
北海公园	Beihai Park
景山公园	Coal Hill Park（Jingshan Park）
十三陵	The Ming Tombs
清东陵	Eastern Royal Tombs of the Qing Dynasty
毛主席纪念堂	Chairman Mao Memorial Hall
人民大会堂	The Great Hall of the People
人民英雄纪念碑	Monument to the People's Heroes
中国国家博物馆（原中国革命博物馆）	National Museum of China
中国历史博物馆	Museum of Chinese History
中国美术馆	The Chinese Art Gallery
卢沟桥	Marco Polo Bridge（Lugou Bridge）
中华世纪坛	China Millennium Monument
首都体育馆	The Capital Gymnasium
国家体育场（鸟巢）	The Beijing National Stadium
北京天文馆	Beijing Planetarium
御花园	Imperial Garden
太和殿	The Hall of Supreme Harmony
中和殿	The Hall of Central Harmony
保和殿	The Hall of Preserving Harmony

养心殿	The Hall of Mental Spring
长春宫	Palace of Eternal Spring
储秀宫	Palace of Gathering Excellence
珍宝馆	Treasures Hall
陶瓷馆	Hall of Pottery and Porcelain
青铜馆	Hall of Bronze
回音壁	Echo Wall
西山八大处	Eight Great Sites in the Western Hills
民族文化宫	The Cultural Palace for Nationalities
鲁迅故居	Luxun's Former Residence
玉佛寺	Jade Buddha Temple
东方明珠塔	Oriental Pearl TV Tower
万国建筑博览	Gallery of International Architecture
外滩	The Bund
上海植物园	Shanghai Botanical Garden
孙中山故居	Dr. Sun Yat-sen's Former Residence
周恩来故居	Zhou Enlai's Former Residence
大沽口炮台	Dagukou Fort
黄花岗七十二烈士墓	Mausoleum of the 72 Martyrs
广州起义烈士陵园	Memorial Mausoleum to Martyrs in Guangzhou Uprising
六榕寺	Temple of Six Banyan Trees
夫子庙	Confucius Temple
中山陵	Dr. Sun Yat-sen's Mausoleum
雨花台	Terrace of the Raining Flowers
世界之窗	Window of the World
锦绣中华	Splendid China
小梅沙	Xiaomeisha Beach Resort
中英街	Chung Ying Street
秦始皇兵马俑	Museum of the Terra-cotta Warriors and Horses of Qin Shihuang
华清池	Huaqing Hot Spring
大雁塔	Big Wild Goose Pagoda
小雁塔	Small Wild Goose Pagoda

碑林	The Museum of Forest of Stone Tablets
钟楼	The Bell Tower
西湖	West Lake
灵隐寺	Temple of Inspired Seclusion (Lingyin Temple)
虎跑泉	Running-Tiger Spring (Hupao Spring)
六和塔	Pagoda of Six Harmonies
千岛湖	Thousand-Island Lake (Qiandao Lake)
苏州园林	Suzhou Gardens
留园	Lingering Garden
拙政园	Humble Administrator's Garden
寒山寺	Hanshan Temple
黄果树瀑布	Huangguoshu Waterfall
泰山	Mount Taishan
避暑山庄	The Imperial Mountain Summer Resort
蓬莱水城	Penglai Water City
天下第一关	The First Pass Under Heaven
庐山	Mount Lushan
南湖	South Lake
天池	Heaven Pool
华山	Mount Huashan
漓江	Lijiang River
桂林山水	Guilin Scenery with Hills and Waters
独秀峰	Solitary Beauty Peak
芦笛岩	Reed Flute Cave
中山公园	Zhongshan Park
黄鹤楼	Yellow Crane Tower
归元寺	Guiyuan Buddhist Temple
龙亭	Dragon Pavilion
大相国寺	Xiangguo Monastery
白马寺	White Horse Temple
龙门石窟	Longmen Grottoes
白云山	White Cloud Mountain
布达拉宫	The Potala Palace
大运河	Grand Canal

滇池	Dianchi Lake
石林	Stone Forest
九寨沟	Nine Village Valley (Jiuzhai Valley)
峨眉山	Emei Mountain
乐山大佛	Leshan Buddha
杜甫草堂	Du Fu Cottage
武侯祠	Temple of Marquis
都江堰	Dujiang Dam
武夷山	Mount Wuyi
鼓浪屿	Gulangyu Islet
观音阁	Goddess of Mercy Pavilion
甘露寺	Sweet Dew Temple
昭君墓	Zhaojun's Tomb
越秀公园	Yuexiu Park
岳阳楼	Yueyang Tower
黄山	Mount Huang (Huangshan)
滕王阁	Tengwang Tower
岳麓书院	Yuelu Academy
马王堆汉墓	Mawangdui Tomb

1. ［英］斯特鲁特. 朗文旅游英语. 南京：南开大学出版社，2007.

2. 穆婷. 旅游英语. 南京：东南大学出版社，2010.

3. 钟灵，曹瑞明，王志芳. 旅游英语. 苏州：苏州大学出版社，2009.

4. 宋美华. 旅游英语. 重庆：重庆大学出版社，2008.

5. 许德君. 旅游英语. 北京：金盾出版社，2004.

6. 郑毅，刘惠波. 旅游英语视听说. 北京：外语教学与研究出版社，2011.

7. 李燕，徐静. 旅游英语. 北京：清华大学出版社，2009.

8. 陈丹. 酒店饭店英语口语实例大全. 北京：中国宇航出版社，2009.

9. 张丽君. 酒店英语. 北京：清华大学出版社，2010.

10. 吴云. 酒店英语. 上海：上海外语教育出版社，2009.

11. 寒春容. 酒店英语. 北京：对外经济贸易大学出版社，2008.

12. 王仰新. 酒店英语. 北京：中国林业出版社，2008.

13. 肖璇，吴建华. 酒店客房英语口语教程. 北京：世界图书出版社，2011.

14. 王远梅. 空乘英语. 北京：国防工业出版社，2010.

15. 王文静. 机场、空乘服务实用英语对话及词汇手册. 北京：水利水电出版社，2009.

16. 王娟. 旅游学. 合肥：合肥工业大学出版社，2009.

教师信息反馈表

为了更好地为您服务，提高教学质量，中国人民大学出版社愿意为您提供全面的教学支持，期望与您建立更广泛的合作关系。请您填好下表后以电子邮件或信件的形式反馈给我们。

您使用过或正在使用的我社教材名称		版次	
您希望获得哪些相关教学资料			
您对本书的建议（可附页）			
您的姓名			
您所在的学校、院系			
您所讲授课程名称			
学生人数			
您的联系地址			
邮政编码		联系电话	
电子邮件（必填）			
您是否为人大社教研网会员	□ 是，会员卡号：＿＿＿＿＿＿＿ □ 不是，现在申请		
您在相关专业是否有主编或参编教材意向	□ 是　　　　　　　□ 否 □ 不一定		
您所希望参编或主编的教材的基本情况（包括内容、框架结构、特色等，可附页）			

我们的联系方式：北京市海淀区中关村大街 31 号

中国人民大学出版社教育分社

邮政编码：100080

电话：010-62515913

网址：http://www.crup.com.cn/jiaoyu/

E-mail：cruplya@126.com